GHOST TALK

GHOST TALK

TRUE CONVERSATIONS WITH THE DEPARTED

ROBERT H. CODDINGTON

Citadel Press
Kensington Publishing Corp.
http://www.kensingtonbooks.com

CITADEL PRESS BOOKS are published by

Kensington Publishing Corp.
850 Third Avenue
New York, NY 10022

Previously published as *Earthbound*

All Kensington titles, imprints, and distributed lines are available at special quantity discounts for bulk purchases for sales promotions, premiums, fund-raising, educational, or institutional use. Special book excerpts or customized printings can also be created to fit specific needs. For details, write or phone the office of the Kensington special sales manager: Kensington Publishing Corp., 850 Third Avenue, New York, NY 10022, attn: Special Sales Department, Phone: 1-800-221-2647

Citadel Press and the Citadel logo are trademarks of Kensington Publishing Corp.

First Citadel Printing: August 2001

10 9 8 7 6 5 4 3 2 1

Printed in the United States of America

Cataloging data may be obtained from the Library of Congress.

ISBN 0-8065-2259-3

FOREWORD

Roger S. Pile, Ph.D.

I am pleased and deeply honored to have been asked to write this foreword for Bob Coddington's new book, *Ghost Talk, True Conversations with the Departed*, particularly since it is a book on ghosts that is long overdue.

While many, many books have been written, and rewritten, on ghosts, there have been none published, to my knowledge, that explore the why of ghosts, the psychology of ghosts, with understanding and objectivity. In *Ghost Talk* are verbatim chronicles, where one can finally see ghosts for what they really are: exhumans.

In the movie *Ghost*, the spirits that came to take Patrick Swayze "home" were points of light—and so they are in reality. Ghosts are not sheets that say, "BOO!" or mindless things that go "BUMP" in the night. They are simply spirit energies that once inhabited bodies and once wore unique physical costumes. We are all spirits on this gigantic stage called Life, costumed for the part we have chosen to play. We make our entrance and our exit. Unfortunately, we may sometimes exit, but fail to leave the stage. Without bodies, spirits often wander the earth in Limbo, having failed upon death to catch the bus home for many different reasons. And so they remain bound to the earth by their own restricted focus.

Death is but a reversal of the birth process, but all of us know that normal procedure can be altered by choice. For example, if one had been told he was going to Hell upon dying, would he want to? Hell no, he won't go! He'll stay right here on the earth. Many die with such guilt that they are unable to accept forgiveness and rescue. Most don't even know they are dead, for they have been programmed to believe that death is a long sleep, a nothing, a blank, or that they will lie in the grave until Gabriel blows a few hot licks on his trumpet. When, after physical death, they still can see, can hear, can think, and have a body of sorts, they become confused—it's the Twilight Zone for them.

I am reminded of an old Yankee farmer who refused to believe he was dead. He said, "I'm here, ain't I? I'm talking to you, ain't I?" I had to admit this was an inescapable logic. When I told him I could prove he was dead, he remained skeptical. He was speaking through a female medium, so I said, "Look at your body!" There was a pause, and then he sighed softly, "Ay, yah, I'm dead." Some ghosts' reactions are unbelievably amusing.

Ghosts have been with us since the beginning of civilization. The concept of life beyond death is pervasive in stories and literature—of both primitive and civilized cultures throughout history. Primitive people spoke to the dead through their priests to request guidance for their problems. In ancient times, back to the Stone Age, tools, pottery, and other items were buried with the dead to help them begin their new life on the other side. Of course, this was carried to extremes in some cultures: in Egypt, servants were buried with their master; in India, until the late 19th century, wives were burned alive on their deceased husbands' funeral pyres. The Greeks buried their dead with a silver coin in the mouth to pay the ferry man, Charon, to take them across the river Styx. A same sort of "gap" exists between this world

and the next in many other religions. e.g., crossing over to Para-
dise, going over the waters to the Happy Hunting Grounds, riding
the skies to Valhalla, etc. These strongly suggest there is simply
a chasm, a dimensional discontinuity, a "vibration" gap between
the visible and invisible worlds.

Fortunately, thanks to extensive research in the Near Death
Experience (NDE), this has been scientifically proven in recent
years. Dr. Raymond Moody, a practicing psychiatrist, says in his
book *Life After Life* that the commonly held idea of death being
an "annihilation,"—an end to consciousness like sleeping or
forgetting—is repudiated by those who have returned from the
dead. Instead, he says, these NDE-ers describe the death experience as a transition, from one state to another, or an entry
into a higher state of consciousness or being. Dr. Kenneth Ring,
Professor of Psychology at the University of Connecticut and a
well-known researcher into the Near Death Experience, in his
book, *Heading Toward Omega,* quotes an NDE-er as saying,
". . . then I noticed that there was a dark area ahead of me, and,
as I approached it, I thought that it was some sort of a tunnel
and immediately, without further thought, I entered into it . . .
and then I went through the tunnel and seemed to be in a
different state. I was in different surroundings. . . ."

Another returnee from the dead told Dr. Ring, "I became aware
of being in a tunnel. I was speeding closer and closer to the light
at the other end." This same gentleman goes on to say that his
experience was like "a rebirth into a higher kind of life." The
tunnel experience has been shown to be very common among
NDE-ers. It would not surprise me a bit if this "tunnel" goes under
the river Styx, replacing the antiquated and very slow ferry. Was
Charon offered early retirement, or was he just laid off? I wonder.

Sadly, in Western civilization, the concept of life after death
has consistently been denied, subverted, twisted, and branded
"heretical." Vigorous and often vicious (substitute "inhuman")

suppression has been exercised by religious authorities and their controlled governments to eradicate such dissident ideas. Origen, a second-century theologian and Church scholar, espoused life after death and reincarnation. Unfortunately, he lacked a sufficient power base, and, in A.D. 543 at the Council of Constantinople, his works were declared heretical. For centuries, just the word "heretic" created terror in large parts of Western civilization. Simply to be *accused* of heresy meant the dungeon or galleys, if one were lucky. Many times the accused heretic, tortured into a confession of heresy to justify the existence of the Inquisition and like bodies, often served as entertainment at such festive occasions as the infamous Spanish auto-da-fé. You may remember that it was the Church which insisted that the earth was flat and that the sun and moon revolved around it; woe betide anyone who said differently, as Galileo found out.

This same mentality exists even in modern times. In the 1700s, Emanuel Swedenborg, a famous and highly respected Swedish statesman, scientist, philosopher, and theologian, published a flood of papers on his experiences and contacts with spirits and the spirit world, on the passage to that world from this one upon physical death, and on the various levels of existence there. What happened? You guessed it! His writings were condemned by the Swedish Church and the Swedish government as heretical and were confiscated and burned. Luckily, his writings had become too widely read and discussed in universities and educated circles throughout Europe to be destroyed or suppressed. Today many believe that Swedenborg heralded a renaissance in the investigation and understanding of life beyond the grave.

Yet ghosts have just kept on popping up; they continued to be discussed and written about. How can such impudence, such defiance of Church authority, be controlled? Heretics were not feared by the populace—they were more to be pitied. But if "ghosts" were made out to be evil, dangerous, even demonic, *they* would be feared! That the religious authorities did their work of damnification well is attested by the fact that here, in our enlightened, highly technological society, ghosts still are looked on as evil, dangerous, and, in some cases, demonic.

Far from their being evil, or demonic, or scary, though, in *Ghost Talk* we become aware that ghosts are like us in the flesh, with unique personalities, concerns, hangups, and psychological dysfunctions. In this book, we are given a rare opportunity to see how mind-sets at the moment of death can strongly influence, if not cause, the postdeath behavior of the ghosts or, as I term them, Earthbounds. My own research over the past twenty years of investigating hauntings and possessions—and doing rescues—includes many situations and conversations similar to those set forth in this book.

What are ghosts really like? Are they different after death than before? Do they have the same attitudes, psychological dysfunctions, mind-sets, fears, obsessions, and the like as when they were in the flesh? Why do they behave as they do? Why do they "haunt"? Are they just trying to get attention the only way they can? Does their mind-set, or belief system, at the moment of death influence or control their postdeath behavior? Is the use of psychotherapy in the postdeath experience more quickly successful than when in physical life? If so, why? Are ghosts, in fact, really like us, with unique personalities, hopes, wishes, fears, longings, guilt feelings, prejudices? These are only some of the questions that have been asked in the twenty years I have been doing research in this field.

By publishing a chronicle of verbatim conversations with many different Earthbounds, Bob Coddington has given those with open and inquiring minds an exceptional, perceptive glimpse of what and who ghosts really are. These cases allow one to see, to feel, and often to understand, the humanity of the Earthbound. They are no longer shadow forms, sheets with eyeholes, ectoplasmic holograms. In this book, they take on character and life. It contains some excellent examples of why we—whether human or ghost—do what we do.

Take the case of Charity MacKenzie. I cite this one, since I was there working with Bob and Marianne, so I can speak with some authority. Charity refused to believe she was dead. To acknowledge her death would have been like acknowledging that *everything* had been taken away from her, including the only security she had left from "this Godforsaken war"—her house. Charity was a Southern lady whose basic security was her husband and their property. But the war had taken the only males in her life—her husband and son. When Richmond burned and her house was on fire, it was simply too much to bear. And so, as we do in physical life when we cannot face reality, she buried it. (As to my bumbling style of questioning, I often pose trick questions or feign ignorance to validate the Earthbound. It's important to know what one is dealing with, as there are other types of non-physical energies about.)

I have worked with Bob and Marianne Coddington and consider them to be totally honest, intelligent, unpretentious, and true People of the Light. Marianne is an exceptional medium, to which I can attest, since I am one myself and I train trance mediums here in Connecticut. Mediums of such integrity and skill are rare, indeed. My ex-wife was such a one. Bob, being an engineer, has presented these conversations in a more scientific manner than I would have, but perhaps that might be better. I think he has produced a very interesting and knowledgeable book.

For those who seek, for those with unfettered minds, for those willing to stretch their imagination, this is a "Must Read" book. It's long overdue. Thank you, Bob and Marianne.

Roger Pile, Ph.D.
Ivoryton, Connecticut

CONTENTS

1. Angelica: A Surprise Encounter — 1
2. Aftermath: Spiritual Inquest — 23
3. Effie: Unaware in Life and Death — 35
4. Charity Ends at Home — 47
5. A Victim of Religious Dogma — 59
6. Children for a Century — 67
7. Afraid of Jesus — 79
8. Shanghaied in Life, Trapped in Death — 95
9. Simon Says, But Child of the Moon Does Not — 111
10. Ghostly Gossips — 127
11. Grounded by Grief — 141
12. Afraid of Hell — 149
13. Missions and Rewards — 169
14. A Ghost of Your Own? — 181
    APPENDIX 1: Resource Organizations — 203
    APPENDIX 2: Bibliography — 207

1
ANGELICA: A SURPRISE ENCOUNTER

The summer night air quivered with a dissonant chorus of insect sounds. In the lawn garden of an elegant home in the Windsor Farms section of Richmond, Virginia, a half-dozen of us drifted idly about in the dusk, our perceptions and senses on the alert for something—anything—unusual. Such as an apparition.

The homeowners' insistence that for many years a ghostly figure in a pink dress was sometimes glimpsed wafting among the trees and shrubs was ample inducement for us, members of a local group bent on probing things metaphysical and psychic, to accept an invitation to visit and explore. None of us had ever before been on a serious "ghost hunt," and each came with his or her own curiosity-driven agenda.

Being something of a technology buff, my focus that night was on what in the literature is called "electronic voice phenomena," the purported capture on audio tape of voices of the dead. With pocket tape recorder running, I was exploring every bower and boundary of the garden, hoping to record something unheard and probably unseen. Others, seeking nothing beyond a glimpse of an incorporeal figure, were scattered about in ones, pairs, and trios.

Rounding a bend in a path in the dusk, I nearly stumbled over Marianne, my wife. She was sitting slouched on the grass, head bowed and eyes closed.

This was curious. Familiar with her several talents for psychic perceptions, I wondered what she was "seeing" that would lead her to sit right there on the ground, and I knelt beside her to ask. As I did, she abruptly began to sob, leaving me momentarily speechless in astonishment and concern. As I groped for suitable words, she faintly moaned something unintelligible between sobs, and suddenly I knew it wasn't Marianne I was hearing! Having read of such things, I understood what was happening: a *disembodied personality of one deceased was controlling her voice*. Never before had Marianne "channeled" a ghost—never had she relinquished her powers of speech to another individual's surviving consciousness. Having absolutely no direct experience with such things, my concern abruptly turned to alarm, verging on panic.

How was I to deal with this clearly distraught stranger who had suddenly displaced my wife's own consciousness and commandeered her voice? How was I to get Marianne back? Was there danger? Is forcible—and prolonged—possession by another spirit truly possible?

I managed enough presence of mind to move the recorder's microphone close to her lips. Softly, I uttered an exploratory "hello."

Her body twitched sharply. Was this a reaction to my voice? "Sorry," I apologized. "I didn't mean to startle you."

The emotional part of my mind was churning with anxiety and doubt, but another part naturally wanted to learn more about this uninvited interloper. "Who's there?" I queried.

The whispered answer was barely audible above the insects' chorus: "I am Angelica."

Well! At least this stranger was hearing me and responding.

I had stumbled onto what we were to learn is a vital first step in interacting with a ghost personality: establishing its name.

Clumsily, I prodded for more. "And who is Angelica?"

I caught a tone of exasperation to her reply. "*I* am Angelica!"

I suspected Angelica was the figure in pink reputed to roam about. "Are you one of the spirits that resides here?"

Her voice grew nearly inaudible. "Am I a spirit? I don't know."

As I pondered my next question, she asked, "Where's Andrew?"

With that, the penny dropped—to use one of Marianne's expressions. I had read of the supposedly "unaware," "earth-bound," or "trapped" soul or spirit—the surviving essence, the consciousness, of a deceased person that somehow is oblivious to the fact of its mortal death and whose awareness is locked in time at that point. This was only an interesting but anecdotal concept to me, until this moment. Now I understood firsthand that such things are real; Angelica was one.

"Andrew?" I asked, to be sure I had heard it right.

Sobbing, "Yes."

Desperately hoping for inspiration or guidance, I asked the obvious: "Who is Andrew?"

"Where is he?" Angelica persisted.

There was no Andrew in our group that night and clearly none within Angelica's purview. I guessed he was a loved one of hers who had died and gone to the next realm. "I think Andrew has gone to better places," I ventured.

She only sobbed inarticulately.

It's difficult to convey in print how convincingly genuine and moving such a manifesting personality can be. How real the pain, how paralyzing the confusion of the ghost's disorientation. As though my anxiety and inexperience weren't enough to deal with, I now suffered the added burden of heartfelt compassion for Angelica. Hoping to comfort her about Andrew, I declared,

"He is happy, and well. More than that I cannot tell you. . . .
And you, Angelica—what can I do to comfort you?"

Sobbing desperately, she said simply, "Find Andrew."

I knew I couldn't find Andrew, but I surmised that she could.
My challenge was to convince her. *"You can go to Andrew,"* I
countered, "did you know that?" But she only sobbed in disbelief.

I pressed on: "You can, because you are free." Not wishing to
say bluntly that she was dead, I gingerly skirted the word. "You
are free of the chains of this physical reality. You have been, for
very long, in our [physical] time."

"I don't understand!"

She still didn't know she was dead, but at least she was opening
up to my efforts. How was I to convince her? "There are other
levels," I declared, "where life is happy, where you can be with
your beloved Andrew, and you can go there, if you but will."

"I've searched for him," Angelica sobbed, in a tone of defeat.

"But you're searching in the wrong place, Angelica."

"He was here," she said.

"Yes, he was here," I conceded, "but that was long ago in our
time."

Angelica suddenly digressed, as though momentarily distracted
by the circumstances of her environment: "Oh, God! The blood,
and the bodies!" Evidently she was surrounded in her frozen
moment of the past by the grisly numbers of the injured and
dead.

"Terrible!" I sympathized. Then, over her sobbing, I pushed
on: "But they do not suffer now. Their souls, Angelica—their
spirits—have gone on to where they are happy and well. Andrew
is with them!"

I pressed my point repeatedly. "And you, Angelica, can follow,
if you but *will* yourself to. Don't trap yourself here; you are free
to go. You are not bound here."

If what I understood of "earthbound" souls was right, this was true. I fervently hoped so. "You have been searching in the wrong place," I continued. "Andrew has gone on to higher planes."

"How do I go?" Angelica asked.

Finally, an opening! "You only need to accept that you are free to go—that you are not bound here."

Still, she doubted. "But he was here!"

"Yes, he was here. And you are *still* here. But your physical existence, Angelica, ended long, long ago." There, I finally said it: she's dead. "And you're free, and you can go to Andrew, and to other loved ones who've gone on, if you but accept that you're free to go."

Her sobs quieted, while she seemed to ponder this new possibility. Grabbing the advantage, I implored, "Just raise your head [symbolically] and look upward. Say 'Andrew, I can come to you, and I will.'"

"He's not here?" She still wasn't wholly convinced.

"He is not here. He is beyond. And he is waiting, and you can go beyond. I must help you to understand—you must understand—that you, too, are free to go beyond, and to find Andrew, *if you but will it in your mind.*"

This was looming as a major challenge. Others had gathered about us in rapt fascination, but none could help. Perhaps I had exulted in the prospect of imminent success too soon.

"Picture in your mind that you are free of this level," I exhorted. "There is nothing holding you here. You *can* go, and you *must!* With God's blessing. Seek and ye shall find. Ask God to show you the way to rejoin with Andrew and your loved ones."

A pause. Silence. Then, at long last, I sensed a subtle change in Marianne's bearing that told me Angelica's energy was leaving her body. "Godspeed, Angelica," I bade her, "We love you, too. Goodbye."

And she was gone. Now my concern turned to Marianne. Would she be herself again, or was a long line of tortured souls waiting to speak in turn? As I watched in trepidation, she straightened and appeared to emerge from her trance.

"I hope you are Marianne," I appealed.

Looking at the those gathered about us, she asked "Why is my face wet?" It indeed was Marianne, much to my relief, puzzled though she clearly was. With her consciousness fully blocked during the entire incident, she didn't know, until I told her, that a ghost had been speaking through her and shedding her tears.

This incident ended well, with the interloping entity moving on and Marianne becoming herself again. Thus began our personal baptism in conversing firsthand with surviving personalities of those who have "passed on." But who was this ghost? When and how did she die? Who is, or was, Andrew? Our brief interchange certainly didn't answer any of these questions. As the next chapter will describe, we can often explore the circumstances leading up to an "earthbound" soul's predicament through psychic sources of knowledge. You will see how we determined that Angelica was a female in desperate search for her Civil War soldier fiancé.

It is our involvement in this and several ensuing ghost encounters that unfolds in this book. Since there must already be hundreds of books devoted to ghost tales, why another? Because this one goes beyond merely reporting observed phenomena or recounting oft told anecdotal tales: this book vividly bares the "life" and reality of its ghost subjects through their own spoken words, as imparted through living persons. Even within the limitations of print, these direct, interactive conversations convey added dimensions of personality and credibility to these accounts.[1]

---

1. The conversations in the following chapters fall far short of polished fictional dialogue because they are taken verbatim, with only minimal editing, from tapes made during the sessions. In the interest of conveying as faithfully as possible the nuances and inflections of actual conversation, much of the mangled syntax,

A basic premise of this book is that "ghosts" do in fact exist. This is beyond question for Marianne (and consequently for me), thanks, in large part, to her gift of aura perception. She not only sees distinctive auras associated with living humans (as well as with porpoises and whales), but also, upon occasion, sees amorphous auras of the disembodied. Being a registered nurse specializing in hospice care, she is sometimes present at the moment of a terminal patient's death, when she sees the vital aura—a diaphanous orb of the individual's life essence—separate itself from the expiring physical body. It's comforting that, on these occasions, without exception in her experience, she perceives a group of other discarnate[2] entities hovering near to welcome the now disembodied but surviving essence of the newly deceased and escort it to its new domain. These perceptions adequately confirm for Marianne and me that, in fact, a nonphysical but conscious and volitional essence of each human being continues to exist beyond physical death. So, of course, we accept the existence of ghostly entities.

We're sharing here some of our experiences with entities we accept as enduring personalities of deceased persons. The dozen or so ghosts introduced here are ones who, for one reason or another, have failed to move on to their intended new domain. It's

repetitions, dead-end digressions, and interruptions—even many (though not all!) of my own gaffes—are included in the transcription.

2. "Discarnate," according to *Webster's* 10th Edition, is an obsolete word meaning "having no physical body." Far from obsolete in metaphysical literature, though, it's widely used as both a noun and an adjective to describe a nonphysical but conscious individuality. Some writers restrict "discarnate" to mean the surviving consciousness of a deceased mortal human and use "entity" for astral or spiritual individualities that presumably have never incarnated. *The Donning International Encyclopedic Psychic Dictionary*, on the other hand, defines a "discarnate entity." The two words—"discarnate" (in its noun sense) and "entity"— are used more or less interchangeably in this book.

true, as Chapter 14 will show, some ghosts (or other nonphysical entities) are opportunistically deceptive, so we can't be absolutely certain of our conclusions, but—given this caveat—we confidently take these ghosts (possibly excepting the one called Peter) to be what, or who, they seem to be.

Some clarification of what I mean by "ghost"—and don't mean—is in order here, since the word is popularly but loosely applied to several different kinds of phenomena.

Survival of the essence (or imprint) of an individual's personality and intellect beyond physical death is a fundamental premise of ghost lore. It is in describing and naming that surviving essence that advocates of ghostly phenomena differ. Some call it an etheric or astral body, or a psychic imprint, an energy matrix, the soul, the spirit, etc. Whatever their terminology, though, they subscribe to the basic concept of a surviving essence that can in some instances interact in various ways with the rest of us in our physical reality.

It must first be said, of course, that none of this is scientific. The topic of ghosts, thus far, has merited little public attention from the academic community of parapsychologists. Being scientists, they prefer to explore more testable aspects of metaphysics, such as remote viewing, ESP, precognition, and psychokinesis, which presumably are amenable to controlled and repeated experiments. Most credentialed parapsychologists presume these aspects to be faculties of the minds of living persons—and since mind seems to them but a function of the organic brain, they are uncomfortable in contemplating a personality's survival of death as a disembodied mind.

Spontaneous ghostly manifestations, though, rarely accommodate laboratory scientists and aren't repeatable on demand. Further, since the academic community is uncomfortable with the very concept of nonphysical intellect, it's a rare parapsychologist who—in professional discourse, at least—can comfortably entertain the popular view of ghosts as more than myth. Mere anecdotal evidence, irrespective of the integrity of its observer, is accorded no scientific stature.

Self-styled parapsychologist Hans Holzer is a noted exception. A prolific writer and diligent field researcher, he taught parapsychology for eight seasons as a professor at the New York Institute of Technology.[3] Holzer accepts the existence of ghosts and has written perhaps more books about them than anyone. Eschewing the sterile laboratory, he says he ". . . prefers competent observers without prejudice . . . working with psychics, healers, and researchers like myself, and letting them 'do their thing' in pleasant surroundings, not in some [sterile] lab with white walls, being told what to do and not to do. Then observe, and learn from what these people do."[4]

After years of firsthand investigation of ghostly matters, usually accompanied by one or another reputed psychic, Holzer asserts, "If what I say—and others like me—is true, then the kind of world that the average person has been taught to believe in is wider and different from what we have been told. It is not a world that ends at physical death; it is not a world where all there is is [just] what we see."

It was in Holzer's books that I read long ago of different classifications of seemingly ghostly happenings. Most recently, we've been seeing and reading Loyd Auerbach, a rare academic parapsychologist brave enough to openly explore and publicly discuss in popular publications the subject of ghosts and his consideration of the *possibility* of a personality's survival of physical death. He, like Holzer, defines distinct categories. In Auerbach's terms, they

3. Credentials given by Holzer in his "Evidence for Life After Death" address at a Psychic Frontiers seminar in Baltimore, on November 29, 1986.

4. *Ibid.* Our own explorations of ghost manifestations closely parallel Holzer's methods.

include "apparitions," "apparitional hauntings," and "poltergeists."[5]

While our prime focus here is on the category of surviving
personalities of the deceased, it's appropriate, for the sake of
clarity, to briefly discuss the distinctions between other "ghostly"
phenomena.

For us, Auerbach's least interesting category is what he terms
an "apparitional haunting." This is a repetitive "psychic movie,"
associated with a given location and perceivable by some individuals, under favorable circumstances. In a typical apparitional
haunting, figures appear to go mechanically through the motions
of an act of violence or to act out a display of some great grief.
The typical scenario reflects a past era, like a belated replay of
some earlier event. It may be just a solitary, nebulous figure slowly
descending a staircase, only to disappear at the bottom, or a
complex scene of opposing forces in noisy battle. Whatever the
content, the sequence of events is identical every time the phenomenon appears, and the ghostly participants are always totally
oblivious to the presence of the observers.

Examples of this type abound among England's countless ghost
traditions. For one, in his *London's Secret History*,[6] Peter Bushell
recounts the tale of a shadowy figure sometimes seen late at night,
standing on a parapet of Hungerford Bridge in London, near a
"haunted" obelisk known as Cleopatra's Needle. It consistently
appears to hesitate in indecision, and then dives off—but vanishes
before it reaches the water below.

5. Loyd Auerbach joined the Core Faculty of the Graduate Parapsychology
Program at John F. Kennedy University, Orinda, California, in 1983, and is author
of *ESP, Hauntings and Poltergeists; Psychic Dreaming; Reincarnation, Channeling and
Possession;* and *Mind Over Matter*. He also frequently appears on the TV program
Sightings and, as of this writing, contributes a regular feature to *Fate* magazine.

6. Bushell, Peter, *London's Secret History* (London: Constable and Company
Limited, 1983).

Characteristic of these repetitive apparitional occurrences are the unchanging sequence of events in each viewing and the total unawareness by the tableau's participants of either the presence or actions of current observers. These hauntings appear to have no cognitive and reactive intellect; they resemble lifeless, mechanical playbacks of an incident somehow recorded in an obscure, astral matrix of space, time, and human experience. While a few apparitional haunting scenarios may revolve around such things as ships, animals, or other nonhuman elements, some researchers believe all hauntings, in this sense of the word, are nothing more than psychic residue left, in the warp and woof of time and space, of intense human emotions triggered in some way by the original incident.

Hauntings of this type are not further addressed in this book. Thus far, they are not a part of Marianne's and/or my experience and—since they reportedly are nothing more than fixed, nonconscious "recordings" in the etheric fabric—they're not subjects of potential interaction, anyway.

For another of his categories, Auerbach embraces the "ghost" term the general public probably is most familiar with: "poltergeist." Occasionally, a reported poltergeist "infestation" will pique the news media and capture national attention, but it's probably mostly thanks to Hollywood that many misperceptions of the subject abound.

Said to mean "noisy ghost," or sometimes "mischievous ghost," poltergeist manifestations include: inexplicable loud noises; floating, falling, and breaking objects; moving furniture; mysteriously opening doors or window; sometimes lights and appliances turning on and off spontaneously; strange smells; and—rarely—alarming outbreaks of flame. Sometimes victims of poltergeist activities glimpse an accompanying apparitional figure.

For instance, Gaither Pratt, an associate of early parapsychological researcher Dr. J. B. Rhine, recounts in his book *Parapsychol-*

ogy, the plight of the Herrmann family in their New York home in 1958. He and fellow researchers investigated sixty-seven incidents of poltergeist activity. These included not only the "usual" spontaneous movements of furniture and small objects, but also the unscrewing of household bottle caps and the untidy spilling of the bottle's contents. With Dr. William Roll, another noted parapsychologist, and a local detective, the researchers investigated and ruled out collective hallucination, radio waves, house vibrations, drafts, plumbing pipes and fixtures, water level variation in a nearby well, possible underground streams, faulty electrical wiring, and takeoffs and landings at a nearby air field. After nearly two months of on-site investigation, Dr. Pratt expressed his conclusion that they were confronted with the "kind of impersonal psychical force which perhaps sometime in the future will fall within the scope of physics. . . ."[7]

Despite the efforts of dedicated debunkers to blame such things on earthquakes, vibration from subways, and other equally untenable rationalizations, poltergeist manipulation of physical objects does exist. Historically blamed on "mischievous" spirits of the dead, in recent years parapsychologists have spawned a different model completely divorced from ghosts. Observation of many cases has led to the conclusion that most—although not all— poltergeist activities are associated not with a fixed locale, but with spatial proximity to a living adolescent. This led to the theory that, in some adolescents, the adjustment to adulthood induces emotional pressures which, if outwardly repressed, may erupt as a subconscious discharge of psychic energies capable of manipulating physical objects. Establishment parapsychology now attributes poltergeist phenomena solely to living human agencies, even though there is as yet no satisfactory explanation for a

7. Cited in Frank Smyth, *Ghosts and Poltergeists* (London: Aldus Books, Limited, 1975).

mechanism by which the mind can directly influence substantial physical objects. (Parapsychologists have a name for it: *psychokinesis*—but not an explanation.) This view conveniently eliminates the scientifically uncomfortable element of nonphysical beings— i.e., ghosts.

Some investigators—Hans Holzer included—reject the living agency limitation of parapsychology's model. It fails in some poltergeist incidents that are more satisfactorily explained in terms of nonphysical initiating sources—incorporeal beings. And why not? So far as I know, no one has yet shown poltergeist activities to deplete the literal energy of a supposed agent's physical body. It follows that if a living person's mind can subconsciously generate forces to manipulate objects without using physical bodily energy, the body is incidental to the process; therefore, a nonphysical mind probably can move objects, too. I'm comfortable with Holzer's contention that some poltergeist phenomena do derive from conscious, but incorporeal, entities.

Poltergeist effects are not yet part of my and Marianne's firsthand experience, though reports of them are peripheral to some of our explorations in this book.

This brings me to the category in which we are experienced, and which is the principal focus of this book. It falls under Auerbach's general heading of "apparitions," sometimes called "spiritualistic" phenomena. To distinguish from his term *"apparitional hauntings,"* Auerbach defines an apparition as "... what is seen, heard, felt, or smelled and is related to some part of the human personality/mind/soul that can somehow exist in our physical universe after the death of the body.... [one that] *has true personality or intelligence behind it.*"[8] [My emphasis.] This broadly defines what I prefer simply to call ghosts throughout the book. Abhorrent though it may be to academia, Marianne and I under-

---

8. *ESP, Hauntings and Poltergeists* (New York: Warner Books, 1986), pp. 22–23.

stand the entities we've encountered to be nonphysical beings having personality, intellect, emotion, volition, and a spiritual nucleus, but rarely do we *see* them as classical apparitions (although Marianne may perceive them as amorphous aura forms). "Ghost" seems the preferable and convenient appellation for Auerbach's apparitions.

It's appropriate to mention, in passing, that not all observed or sensed specters are the essences of once-mortal humans. Occasionally, a perceived nonphysical, apparitional figure is projected in some fashion by a *living* person. ("Bilocation" and the "doppelganger" are intriguing subjects beyond the scope of this book.) Too, it's our understanding that beings exist in the nonphysical realms—perhaps theology's angels or mysticism's spirit guides, for instance—which have never existed as physical humans but which nevertheless may interact with our reality. However, we understand that all the ghosts introduced in the succeeding chapters once occupied human bodies.

There are differences even among these, explored more fully in their corresponding chapters. Briefly summarized, some remain interactive on our plane by choice. At least one was "restrained" by grieving family members; another feared infernal punishment; while most—of which Angelica was a prime example—were what we call "unaware," "trapped," or "earthbound" souls. It's inexplicable, but widely accepted among researchers of ghost phenomena, that some personalities simply aren't aware they have physically died and need to be convinced they are free to move on to more appropriate realms. Our experience seems to confirm this.

The usual explanation for such unawareness is that the death was sudden and unforeseen, through trauma or an abruptly fatal turn of illness—or was so hysterically resisted—that the subject's consciousness simply rejected, or blanked out, the fact. (Conversely, hospice patients, by definition, are terminally ill and aware of probable death within six months; of course they're prepared for their transition.)

As you saw with Angelica, to converse directly with these ghosts, we use the ancient technique of "mediumship." The modern euphemism for direct verbal mediumship is "channeling," which now includes the manifesting of supposedly exalted beings, space entities, or deities, though earlier mediums communicated in various ways with only deceased humans. Even though fraud, rampant among professed mediums early in this century, pushed the word mediumship into disrepute, I consider it still appropriate when working with ghosts, as we define them here.

Verbal mediumship is a process by which a person so gifted—the medium—enters a mental state in which her or his own consciousness steps aside, so to speak, and allows an external, disembodied consciousness to act through the medium's physical body. This is done only with suitable precautions, such as prayer or invoking a psychic shield; just as in the physical realm, there are always imposters and opportunists in the nonphysical realms poised to deceive the unwary.

"Mediumship" suggests to many the stereotypical seance circle of seekers anxiously holding hands in a dark room, arcane incantations, "ectoplasm," trumpets or megaphones, and the other trappings of the "physical" mediums of decades ago. Not so. The channeling of discarnate personalities by a mediumistic psychic can and does occur in very ordinary social settings. It usually occurs only upon conscious invitation by the medium, although it can happen spontaneously (presumably with the medium's permission on some level), when pertinent to do so, as was the case with Angelica's emergence.

Another point of clarification here: the personalities channeled by authentic mediums are *not* alternate figments of their own personalities. Unlike the subject of the film *The Three Faces of Eve* and others, mediums are not suffering from Multiple Personality

Disorder (MPD). MPD is a recognized psychological condition in which the subject's own mind evolves two or more distinct, dissociated personalities, which may or may not be aware of one another. Such personalities tend to be shallow, like incompletely fleshed out fictional characters, and they usually reappear from time to time. In contrast, one who intimately knows a medium and has observed her or him channel numbers of convincingly real personalities recognizes them as external to the medium, beyond doubt. Too, those manifesting as ghosts that finally move on, never reappear.[9]

Why must we resort to mediumship? In theory, at present, an aware ghost can hear us when we simply speak aloud, so if we just conversationally ask it to move on, it should understand and respond (which an aware one *may* do). But as Angelica, and many of those in later chapters, illustrates, many ghosts seem dreamlike, to be oblivious to current external reality.

Doubtless you've had dreams during which you're unaware of ordinary external sounds, and it takes something highly intrusive—the alarm, the telephone, or a loud voice—to interrupt them. That sound may at first even be integrated briefly into the scenario of your dream, before it penetrates as external reality, and you suddenly realize you had been dreaming. The "unaware" ghost seems to be similarly immersed in its own repetitive nightmare of events, now past, oblivious to present reality. It is into this obsessive dream that the "medium" can ingratiate himself

9. Certain religious factions adhere rigidly to a belief that the surviving human soul becomes utterly dormant and unknowing at the instant of physical death, to revive only at Judgment Day. These factions accept the reality of discarnate beings and validity of mediumship, but they believe all such manifestations to be Satanic or demonic imposters bent upon deceiving mankind. It's true that we have confronted an occasional deceitful and opportunistic discarnate, but most of those of our acquaintance are only disoriented and confused—not demonic. It's our conviction that by facilitating the "release" of confused surviving human souls, when the occasion arises, we are performing a spiritually positive service.

or herself as a channel. You will find most ghosts in this book first perceived me and other questioners as manifesting in their own scenarios, and our challenge was to convince them that they were locked in a dream from which they could willfully awaken and move into their own plane of reality. This requires a persuasive give-and-take of fully verbal dialogue to clarify things for them.

Marianne is the principal medium for most of our experiences, and I am the usual interviewer of the channeled personalities. (Marianne commonly has no memory of the words that pass her lips during a mediumistic trance and must listen to the session tape to learn what happened.) We usually are accompanied by other experienced psychics and investigators from our circle of metaphysical researchers. Some of our sessions are unique in that a second person may drop into trance to accommodate a deceased relative or friend of the target ghost who comes to guide it onward.

How does it happen that we—Marianne and I—have become involved with these ghosts? Who are we? Here's a brief background:

I am native to the Midwest, a product of small, rural towns, a stint on my grandfather's farm, and even a couple of pupil years in a one-room country school. My academic study, following wartime military service, culminated in a B.S. in Physics. My first career spanned a quarter-century in radio and television broadcasting in seven assorted states, out of which came my first book, *Modern Radio Broadcasting*.[10] When broadcasting became no longer fulfilling to me, I switched to a second career, using my facility with words as a technical writer for an international manufacturing firm.

From childhood observation of my mother's occasional psychic perceptions, I've always supposed there was a greater reality than

10. Blue Ridge Summit, Pennsylvania: TAB Books, 1969.

the eye normally perceives, and I long enjoyed hearing and reading of others' psychic and metaphysical experiences. When grown children and an ended marriage left me with time on my hands, I moved from mere passive observation to joining groups engaged in active study and experiential confirmation of concepts of the paranormal.

It was to one of these groups that Marianne, a native northern Virginian, came several years ago. As one of her mentors, I soon discerned her uncommon degree of intuitive perception, which we undertook to hone together. (We also discovered that, despite our age difference, we had many other interests and values in common, and we soon formed our personal subgroup of two by marrying.)

As Marianne grew to understand and focus her talents, she learned to interpret her aura perceptions and to trust her intuitive insights, when counseling others. The spiritual aspect of the psychic drew her to the nursing profession, whereupon she returned to college and ultimately became a registered nurse, now specializing in hospice nursing—the care of the terminally ill.

When the metaphysical study group began degenerating under its charismatic founder into a cult, Marianne and I joined a handful of other concerned members and broke away to form our own group, the Metaphysical Research Group (MRG), of Richmond, Virginia. Probably the most dogma-free metaphysical organization in the country, it has survived in modest numbers for well over a decade.

From our participation in MRG and various seminars and symposia, as well as personal explorations of many facets of metaphysics, we are visible among the local community of seekers. Marianne has grown psychically through her occasional intuitive counseling for friends, in person or by telephone, and spiritually by interacting professionally with numbers of dying patients. Out of my experiences, observations, and conclusions, I have written columns and articles for local, regional, and national periodicals, and, finally, my book *Death Brings Many Surprises*,[11] a primer of metaphysical concepts for the fledgling seeker. I consider myself not a metaphysician—the usual self-styled designation—but a metaphysicist, which I define as one whose focus is more on the mechanisms through which paranormal events occur than on their results.

Others also figure often in the episodes related here. Charles Strickland is a materially successful local businessman who, pursuing personal growth, joined the Metaphysical Research Group several years ago and rapidly discovered, developed, and focused his several psychic gifts. He also served several terms as the group's president, during which MRG grew from a dedicated handful meeting in private homes to a viable organization that meets in public rooms to hear guest speakers and exchange experiences and viewpoints. Among other accomplishments, he is a talented psychic trance counselor.

Lou Ebersole came to MRG with her ability to divine information psychometrically, i.e., by holding a client's personal item and receiving from it psychic impressions pertinent to its owner. She subsequently found she could "channel" her Higher Self[12] and other entities in trance. Between her publishing and public relations consultancy, Lou circulates widely among the local business community and, through her contacts, has brought others— including Charles Strickland—to MRG.

Lou's adult son, Don, also participated in one episode here. An adventurous, widely traveled young man, Don inherited some of his mother's psychic sensitivity.

Sandie Fairhill and her husband, Phil, are fellow cofounders,

11. New York: Ballantine/Ivy Books, 1987.

12. Our concept of one's Higher or Superconscious self and its role in channeling is discussed in the following chapter.

with Marianne and me, of our Metaphysical Research Group. Sandie is a transplant from New England who set out several years ago to visit the late Edgar Cayce's Association for Research and Enlightenment in Virginia Beach, Virginia, and settled in Richmond. A registered nurse having several psychic talents, she is an excellent trance "reader" and channeler, in close attunement with her Higher Self and the insights she gains from it.

Phil Fairhill is a New Jersey native whose imposing, no-nonsense appearance—and federal law-enforcement occupation—hides his considerable psychic abilities, which he feels he inherited from his mother and her ancestry. With a longtime interest in—and study of—human health, he is highly adept at intuitive diagnosis of a subject's physical dysfunctions. Too, being closely attuned to his Higher Self, he is skilled in sensing and evaluating the forces at work in paranormal events.

Roger Pile, Ph.D., is a highly experienced student, practitioner, writer, and teacher of metaphysics, regionally well-known in the New England metaphysical community. He visited Richmond in 1985, conducting classes and pursuing his self-appointed mission of releasing "earthbound" souls, including two chronicled here.

Of course those individuals who have been host to ghostly phenomena are also principal participants in their respective episodes. They are identified, pseudonymously when appropriate, in their related chapters.

As you saw, our first encounter was spontaneous and unexpected; it was also witnessed by several group members. Having thus acquired in their eyes some minor note as local "ghost busters," we occasionally are approached by people who suspect ghost presences in their homes and who wish confirmation, at least, or more often release, of their discarnate residents.

There's a practical reason for the regional locus of our experiences: because we live and work in Richmond, the radius of our metaphysical excursions is perforce limited to the central Virginia area. Since most ghosts seem to focus their presence near their geographical locations of death—and many died a century or more ago—it's not surprising that some of our ghosts relate to the Civil War era. Others, though, range from the 1400s to late in this century. Thus, these ghost experiences collectively give glimpses, through ostensibly firsthand accounts, of facets of life in the geographical heart of the Confederacy at widely differing times. Join us through the following chapters in our initiation to and growth in the mysterious realm of responsive ghosts.

2

AFTERMATH: SPIRITUAL INQUEST

Relating our Angelica experience was the sensation of the evening, as the group gathered on the back porch afterward. I saw an elderly lady—the owner who invited us to explore the grounds, but who wasn't really comfortable with the thought of ghosts—peering out a window at the gathering. But all eyes were on Marianne, as she related her reactions to the ordeal.

And an ordeal it was, to a degree. "When I first came out of trance," she related, "I felt emotionally drained without knowing why. I felt confusion—disorientation—and a sense of time loss. I also had a sense of some kind of catharsis, but I couldn't define it. Too, I was curious about why Bob looked so worried."

And I certainly had been. From the moment I realized that Marianne was in trance, under the control of another personality, I had been deeply concerned for her physical well-being and was anxious about restoring her to her own consciousness. It must have shown on my face when Marianne regained normal consciousness, even in the near-darkness.

"What happened to make you go into trance?" someone asked.

"While I was walking around at random, I kept feeling drawn

to that spot near the bridal wreath bush. I went back there and sat down to "open up" briefly to [her Higher Self] to find out why I was being guided there. I didn't mean to go into deep trance. I said the first few words of my [trance-inducing] mantra— and the next thing I recall, I was sitting there with tears running down my face and Bob looking worried.

"[From aura perception] I already accepted the existence of ghosts.[1] Although I was aware of an entity here, I did not expect it to come through me; when I sat down on the lawn, it was only with the expectation that I would receive some sort of insight from my Higher Self as to who the entity was. So I was very surprised when I came out of the trance state with my body feeling very physically shaken—very tight, tense muscles around the neck and shoulders. I was aware of my face being wet, and I had that feeling of being drained one gets after a very emotional experience.

"The loss of time was upsetting. Losing control of my memory for that long is perhaps the most distressing aspect of this experience.[2] In retrospect, I suppose I did give my Higher Self permission to work with me on this one, and it's my understanding that it just stepped aside to allow Angelica to come through.

"As for the [channeled] information that came through, since I 'wasn't there,' my retrospective isn't any more useful than anyone else's."

We played the tape and replayed portions of it many times, as we sought to understand what had happened. As Marianne listened, she found herself very detached from it, as though someone else were speaking. She knew it to be her voice, yet the

1. The Angelica episode preceded Marianne's hospice experience, wherein she perceives the separation of a surviving life essence from its physical body at death.

2. Since such memory gaps often occur while she is channeling a ghost, Marianne since has become accustomed to the resulting sense of time loss.

content was strange to her, and the cadence of the speech wasn't her own. It was Angelica's.

But the scenario captured on the tape was tantalizingly incomplete. Who was Angelica? And Andrew? What had happened to leave Angelica's consciousness frozen in time—and when?

Much about a ghost's immediate predicament—and most of those we engage *are* in a predicament—can be deduced from our direct conversation with it. However, there's usually much unsaid, as in this episode. We've since learned to ask for more details directly from the ghost while it's manifesting, but, even at best, much is left unsaid.

For more information, we often call upon psychics in our group to discern and flesh out the circumstances, events, and people in the ghost's physical life, which culminated in its predicament. This helps us to better understand our experience in broad perspective.

It's appropriate here to explain our understanding of how such collateral information can be psychically accessed. Marianne and I, and many of our associates, embrace the concept that each of us has an exalted plane of consciousness—an individual and unique Higher Self we call the Superconscious—conveniently dubbed the "SC"—which is a cosmically aware spiritual aspect of the individual herself or himself, and is the true source of most psychic abilities. The SC is a complete, distinct intellect by itself and has its own personality. While in our active, conscious state, we may have no more cognizance of this higher mind than of our subconscious mind, it nevertheless can and often does subtly guide us during moments of attunement.

(Some call this innate source of guidance and knowledge a spirit guide and others call it a guardian angel, although one also may have associated spirit guides and guardian "angels" that are separate entities.)

This personal superconscious mind ordinarily functions in the timeless and spaceless realm of the nonphysical—perhaps, with apologies to Jung—the realm of the Collective *Super*conscious. At this level, it can communicate telepathically across our time and space with other SC's and thereby access information from those of other individuals and, perhaps, also from a dynamic repository of human history such as the so-called Akashic Records. (This concept also posits the SC to be the seat of our spirituality, being that facet of mind through which we may receive inspiration and enlightenment from higher spiritual sources. It would take an entire volume to fully depict the characteristics of the Superconscious, as we understand them, which I did some years ago in my book *Death Brings Many Surprises*.)

While this higher level of mind usually works beneath (or above) our normal consciousness, it may be accessed more directly through appropriate meditation. Moreover, some individuals learn to set aside normal consciousness in trance and allow their SC to literally speak in dialogue with other persons. This, too, is channeling or mediumship, differing only in that the entity speaking is not an external, discarnate being such as a ghost or a supposedly enlightened "spirit guide," but is in fact the higher consciousness of the channeler or medium herself or himself.

It is from such superconscious sources that we acquire some of the background information to flesh out what we learn from direct ghost interactions. You will see in succeeding chapters how we frequently called on Marianne and others to channel direct information from their SC's so we may better understand our experiences.

On this night, we turned to psychic Sandie Fairhill (introduced in the previous chapter) for more information on the circumstances of Angelica's predicament. Assenting, she slipped into trance to access and channel her Superconscious. To paraphrase, this is what her SC related:

The site of the lawn garden was that of a temporary field hospital during some stage of the Civil War. Andrew was a wounded Confederate officer treated in the hospital, and Angelica was his seventeen-year-old fiancée who, when she learned Andrew was among the hospital's patients, had ventured from her Richmond home to comfort him.

The hospital, improvised from tattered tents and rickety cots and having few medical necessities available, was greatly overcrowded with wounded and dying soldiers, "almost stacked like cordwood." Short-staffed, the doctors, nurses, and assistants were stressed to the point of exhaustion.

Upon her arrival, Angelica wished to immediately start searching among the wounded for her beloved Andrew, but she was pressed into improvising bandages and quenching patients' thirst. While she was so occupied, she was told Andrew had succumbed to his wounds before her arrival.

Angelica adamantly refused to accept this news. She simply could not believe, on the emotional level, that Andrew would die without saying goodbye to her. Stressed by the bloodshed and overwhelming misery, shocked by the report of Andrew's death, and unstrung by emotional conflict, her coordination suffered and she stumbled over a body. She fell on a sharp instrument, described by Sandie only as "something similar to a bayonet," and died almost immediately, Andrew's name on her lips.

Marianne had verbally channeled her own SC in trance upon occasion for many years, before she channeled Angelica, her first ghost. When discussing her channeling, she said, "Probably the biggest difference I experience is that I am normally—probably ninety-five percent of the time—aware of everything that's going on, when I'm channeling my own SC; with ghosts, most of the time I am unaware of what's going on while it's happening.

Usually, listening to the tape afterwards [the content] comes as something of a surprise. But I often sense a "different energy"— a foreign one—when an external personality is given control.

"I don't look for any insight or wisdom from a ghost, as I do from my SC. A ghost is very much caught in its own time frame and its own agenda. When I'm in such a trance, it's up to the interviewer, usually my husband Bob, to persuade a confused ghost to 'break out' and move on."

The usual explanation for the failure of an unaware soul to realize it has passed from the physical plane is that its death was so sudden and traumatic that the victim's conscious mind (the part that hangs onto this plane) can't—or won't—grasp what happened. Its focus remains on whatever it was intensely seeking at the moment of death.

This postulate gives us pause for thought. Where, for instance, is a welcoming committee of discarnates such as Marianne sees at the death of hospice patients (most of whom have already accepted the imminence of death)? Does a sudden and untimely death catch the astral welcomers unprepared? Does it require some interval on their indeterminate time plane to gather to greet and lead the newcomer to their realm? Or—as postulated above—is the victim's pre-death obsession so compelling that the surviving consciousness totally blocks its own Higher Self and is oblivious, as well, to guiding discarnates who may already be present at the fatal moment?

Be that as it may, numerous cases of a departed's timeless ignorance of his or her own death do exist in the literature. Angelica, focusing every shred of her emotional energy on her search for Andrew, died abruptly at the height of her obsession, and that obsession continued unchanged and unresolved for over a hundred years of our present physical reality. The mortally wounded Andrew, however, presumably had died aware and made a normal transition to the next realm, where we understand Angelica—with our help—finally joined him.

The "unaware" soul concept challenges some facets of our concept of the Superconscious. As one of our early mentors used to question, if in fact each of us has a superconscious level of mind with its cosmic knowledge, how can a physically deceased personality be "unaware" of its status? Surely its SC is aware of the mortal's physical death and, being the presumably superior level of consciousness, one would expect it to overcome and dispel the earthbound fixation of its satellite conscious mind. Ordinarily, the conscious mind should merge upon death with its SC to integrate the total being into a single, composite, and cosmically aware entity.

Yet we are told by our own SC's that a deceased individual's SC can be frustrated by its by total inability to break through and get the "attention" of its earth-fixated mortal consciousness. How does this happen?

We understand the answer lies in the focus of conscious free will. All of us sometimes volitionally do something contrary to "our better judgment," and when one becomes obsessively consumed by intense emotion, one is totally oblivious to one's innate "better judgment," from whatever level of consciousness, and becomes fixated. Evidently some circumstances of sudden or untimely death can lock the surviving consciousness in a riveting fixation that can't be penetrated by the deceased's Higher Self.

It's not difficult to envision how this communication block could occur. Most of us have, at one time or another, become so engrossed—so intensely focused—in reading, or on a TV program, or in a daydream, as to be completely unaware of someone calling or speaking to us. If concentration on a mere book or sports program can shut out strong external signals on the conscious level, it's not a big stretch to suppose that an all-consuming focus at the conscious level on impending, violent death, for example, would close off that consciousness to the subtle signals from other levels of mind. When that focus festers into a conscious-level, all-consuming timeless obsession, it's like a computer becoming locked into a repetitive, meaningless cycle (as sometimes happens) which requires drastic measures to interrupt. Toward this end, we have found, the deceased's SC often arranges, on some cosmic level, for a channeler to offer voice to the ghost, and, as we have found, it may even recruit the surviving energy of a deceased loved one to manifest itself to the newly "released" consciousness to lead him/her to the next realm.

As implied above, we understand that our ghost encounters don't come about by pure chance. We've been told (by our SC's) more than once that the frustrated SC of an "unaware" has taken roundabout action by enlisting Marianne's and other involved SC's to guide us, however subtly, into situations leading to "rescue" encounters.

When research time permits, we occasionally succeed in at least partially verifying psychically gleaned data through existing records. In most cases, though, just the information inferred from the verbal interchange with the ghost adequately explains its predicament and, if it helps in a successful soul "rescue," its literal validity is immaterial to our purpose. Any subsequent research seeking confirmation is purely for our own curiosity and satisfaction.

There is an interesting aspect to our exploration of the Angelica story. One of our group there, a lady of local social stature and long Richmond experience, heard a familiar note in the information coming to light in this episode. She believed it fit a legendary—and apparently apocryphal—account handed down in Richmond circles since the Civil War. It seems a young woman, affectionately nicknamed "Angelica" by her physician father, because of her halo of golden hair, was betrothed to a Confederate officer who was the son of a prominent Richmond family. When she heard he had been injured in battle and taken to the improvised hospital, so the story goes, Angelica became determined to find and care for him but met with a fatal accident at the hospital site instead. It should be noted that Marianne, Sandie, and I are not native to Richmond, and were entirely unfamiliar with this local legend, until it was told to us *after* Angelica's manifestation and Sandie's trance-sourced account.

Exploring first whether the site of the Angelica incident might have been one of an improvised Civil War hospital revealed that nearly all of Richmond was pressed into emergency care. As historian Alfred Hoyt Bill[3] puts it: "Wounded men . . . filled tobacco warehouses, even stores. . . . Private drawing rooms became emergency wards.

"Every house, it seemed, was either a hospital or the abode of mourning. . . . There was not enough of anything. Bandages, lint [cotton], stretchers, beds, and bedding all were exhausted. Many died of the mortification of their wounds because essential care could not be given to all in time to save them."

Bill's words even underscore our perception of Angelica's quest: "Among them [the wounded] flitted white-faced women searching for a brother, husband, lover, or son." Certainly this conforms to our understanding of Angelica's actions at the time of her death.

We have since learned—as later chapters will confirm—that one need not be physically present at the site of a ghost's demise in order to make contact. Thus, it's immaterial whether our Windsor Farms location was specifically that of a field hospital; certainly—with more than sixty hospitals in the city during the

---

3. Alfred Hoyt Bill, *The Beleaguered City* (Westport, Connecticut: Greenwood Press, 1946, 1980).

peak years, and many stores, warehouses, and homes pressed into impromptu hospital duty—we couldn't have been far from one. We now know that even if the site were not the actual location of a hospital, this would not invalidate Angelica's story.

But the only specific details we had from Angelica were their names. Now, "Angelica" and "Andrew" aren't sufficient for searching historical records by name, and I have been unable to find the legend told us that night by the lifelong Richmond resident preserved in print. Since we now are out of touch with the lady, we're at an impasse, and there the incident rests for now.

So, as we find frequently happens, hard confirmation of psychically obtained information proves more difficult to establish than our limited time and resources can accommodate. It's tantalizing—and not uncommon—to find evidence hinting at validity but falling disappointingly short of satisfactory proof. This elusiveness may result simply from skimpy historical records; conversely, I concede there may be a deeper significance that calls for delving into the phenomenon further. This issue will surface again in succeeding chapters.

By way of a parenthetical postscript: In the excitement of coping with our unexpected visitor, I was distracted from my original quest for capturing a ghostly voice with the tape recorder, but I left it running for parts of our animated discussion following Angelica's release. Upon playing the discussion tape later, I was struck by what seem to be two isolated, whispered words virtually buried in the night noises. They are so ephemeral as to be controversial; I and certain others can discern—or imagine—them, always at the same spot on the tape, while still others detect nothing at that position, distinct from the general noise. It's almost as if the night noises themselves were modulated to mouth the words "I know!" at a point in the discussion where they would be a fitting interjection by a listener to the conversation. No living person said it, nor did Angelica—but we understand there to be a number of other earthbound entities associated with that location. Did we have a ghostly kibitzer whispering into my recorder?

3

EFFIE: UNAWARE IN LIFE AND DEATH

In the early 1980s, Janet[1] was living with her husband and their two young children in a rambling, three-story house in a Virginia town of perhaps a hundred residents. It's a house that grew, wing by ell, over the centuries. Part of it dates to the 1790s, with additions in 1842 and 1880. It's certainly old enough to be respectably haunted,[2] but no one told them it was when Janet and her husband bought it. Perhaps no one knew. In 1983, it became the site of a notable milestone in our education and the most moving episode of our early ghost experiences.

Janet and Marianne were then coworkers in the same institution. In the course of their acquaintance, Janet discovered Marianne's interest in hauntings and told her of certain mysterious experiences in Janet's two-century-old home. Marianne eagerly arranged to meet socially with her to hear the details.

A small group of us gathered a few days later. After introduc-

1. A pseudonym; also, some details have been changed to preserve "Janet's" anonymity.
2. A house needn't be old to be the locus of ghost infestation. Even brand new ones sometimes shelter invisible residents.

tions, Janet told us she and her family had lived in the house about six years, during which she'd always had mostly a "good feeling" about it. But, while she'd never been fearful of it, she and her husband had occasionally heard noises they couldn't account for, such as doors closing mysteriously; hearing in the middle of the night what sounded like a music box playing on the third floor; and sometimes there seemed to be a woman talking. But the most distressing and puzzling sound was that of a baby crying.

With retiree neighbors having no infants or small children, and not even a neighborhood cat whose yowls could be misinterpreted, she found the baby sounds particularly baffling—especially because they seemed to come from the upper floors of the rambling house. By the time she or her husband would run upstairs to check, all was quiet.

Janet went on to describe the two little rooms with dormer windows on the third floor, in which, after the rooms' renovation, she planned to put her son and daughter. One of these rooms, though, seemed to Janet to have an inexplicably cold and uncomfortable atmosphere, while the other, just across the hall, really "felt good."

More sinister, though, was a sensation Janet repeatedly felt at the top of the third floor staircase. When she descended, she said, she sensed "something" behind her—something like a tall shadow, causing her to firmly grasp the banister, lest the "something" should somehow push her off balance.

None of these sensations occurred when her husband was in the room with her. Only when she was there alone did she feel "really strange." So Janet tried to dismiss them as just her imagination—until her visiting sister revealed that she, too, sensed something foreboding in the room and urged Janet not to house her son there. This independent confirmation of "something there" reinforced Janet's misgivings.

To us, Janet's story suggested that the house did indeed have one or more incorporeal residents. The result of our meeting was an invitation to investigate it. Marianne and I, perhaps overconfident after surviving our initial ghost contact, Angelica, eagerly assented.

It was just three days before all-haunts day, Halloween, when a group of us, including several who are psychically sensitive, descended on the house. Touring it, we noted the differences in construction of the various building periods of the house. Janet related how, while renovating some areas, they had discovered names and dates penciled on beams and timbers, from which they inferred the ages of the various structural additions.

After exploring the lower floors, we headed up to *the* room— the one in which Janet and her sister felt an oppressive emotional climate. The stairway to the third floor rose steeply from the ninety-degree turn of its bottom steps, and we ascended with particular care.

We emerged into a hallway with cheerful looking rooms with dormer windows opening off it. Janet led us into one on the left. This, she told us, was *the* room.

Marianne stepped to the center of the room and paused, figuratively sniffing the atmosphere psychically. "Something's happened in this area," she concluded. "There's something in here. And I felt something on the stairs, too, on about the fifth or sixth step from the top."

"I did, too," confirmed Bonnie, another of the sensitives among us.

"What's it feel like?" someone asked.

Marianne struggled with the old challenge of verbally describing psychic impressions. "A feeling of . . . of a disturbance; that's the best way I can put it," she concluded. "Not scary, really, but heavy . . . it's *unhappy.*"

Feel? Considering her usual aura perception, I was expecting her to *see* something. "But don't you *see* anything?" I wondered aloud.

"In here, no. But I'm certainly aware of a presence of some sort." Thus, we learned that, for whatever her Higher Self's reasons, Marianne doesn't always see lingering discarnates, though she may otherwise sense their presence.

The logical next step was to seek contact with the discarnate source of the unhappy energy. Marianne sat lotus-style on the roughhewn floor, and I knelt in front of her with a microphone in my hand and butterflies in my stomach. The others gathered about us in apprehensive but rapt attention, and we waited for her to go into trance.

Only moments later, I saw the subtle shift in her posture and vitality, signifying that Marianne's consciousness had relinquished control, so that another might "wear" her body. Her body began the shaking and shuddering, which I have learned often heralds the entry of a foreign personality.

For most discarnates, having been bodiless for many years, physicality is a strange, like-new experience. Some entering personalities spend long minutes in silence, feeling arms, legs, face, and hands in detail, learning to manipulate a strange body— perhaps even adjusting to one of the opposite sex from the last one.

Speaking is the greatest challenge to physical coordination, and an emerging entity may grunt, groan, and stammer awhile, before managing to speak intelligibly through the medium's body. While some give up and never speak, most "unaware" ones of our experience will persist, being driven in their obsession by an urgent desire to communicate their plight.

There was a long silence. I waited, weighing the promise of adventure against dread of the unknown. Then Marianne's entire body abruptly lurched with intense sobbing. Even though I knew Marianne was not consciously experiencing this emotional agony,

I was concerned about the physical aftereffects of the stress on her body.

I tried to comfort this personality. Being yet a novice at spirit releases, I thought a technique sometimes used by hypnotists to calm their subjects—a suggestion to mentally step aside from subjective participation in the perceived situation and view it merely as an objective spectator—might work.

"It's all right," I said in what was intended to be a tone of assurance. "Release! Step aside and just see yourself without emotion. It's all right."

I may as well have been addressing a cinder block. The sobbing continued, unabated. This entity was inconsolable and clearly not susceptible to suggestion. (We've since concluded that all obsessively unaware entities aren't receptive to the "objective viewpoint" approach.) Waiting, I pondered my next move.

Suddenly words came—anguished words, uttered between sobs: "She gonna kill me!" This personality sounded female and old South black.

"No, she's not!" I could say this confidently to a ghost.

Not convincingly, though. Again, she blurted, "The missus is gonna kill me!" She was deadly serious, this ghost. She wasn't using "kill" in a figurative sense at all; she was in fact desperately fearful for her very life—not realizing she already was dead.

She said it several more times, utterly oblivious to my efforts to allay her terror. I began to fear that I had been thrust into a situation beyond my ability to resolve. I just knelt there, momentarily speechless and helpless.

Then, as she spoke again, a picture finally began to emerge. "I done ever'thing I could," she lamented, amidst her sobs. "The baby, he had jaundice since the day he was birffed."

"And you're being blamed for its death?" I ventured.

"I gave him the arrowroot," she sobbed, "just like the doctor told me. When she comes home and finds that baby dead, she gonna kill me."

How could I assure her that her mistress was not going to kill her, when for all I knew thus far, that could in fact be what had happened. How could I penetrate her agitated state and lead her to the realization of her true state?

As I pondered this, she sobbingly explained further: "He the only boy child. Missus, she cain't have no mo'."

It occurred to me here—belatedly—to ask her name.

"Effie," she blurted between sobs.

"Effie?" I had her repeat it to be sure I had it right.

"And," I continued, "what is the year?"

"I don't know."

It's hard to imagine today that anyone past the age of eight or ten wouldn't know the year, but perhaps it's not unreasonable to suppose that, to a family's domestic in earlier times, the date may have had little significance. I took this to be the case with Effie.

The story unfolded further. "I told her the baby was sickly," Effie said. "I done watched him." She spoke haltingly, between sobs. "He done whined and whined and whined and wailed. . . . Then I come in and he was gone!" More sobs, then she reiterated her fear: "When she comes, she gonna kill me!"

To hear these actual words on the tape—to hear this tormented soul pouring out grief-stricken remorse over the death of her charge and whimpering in fear for her own life can bring tears to one's eyes, even now. At the time she uttered them, they were intensely moving.

I knew there *must*, in some way, be a wedge to penetrate Effie's fixation. I fired another question: "Have you been waiting long for her to come home?"

"I don't know." Apparently time wasn't significant to Effie, either.

"Why are you here?"

Again, "I don't know."

I surely seemed to be getting nowhere. Somehow, I *had* to find a key to bring her up to the present. "Effie," I said, "let me tell you something: what happened has happened long, long ago."

"No, suh!" She was adamant.

We did a "yes"–"no" exchange for a couple of rounds, then I pressed on. I recalled from my early experience that suggesting direct access to heaven or God may get through to an unaware soul. "You're among friends now, Effie," I pressed on, "but you do not belong on this plane. You can go *home*. Tell me, do you believe in God? Do you pray to God?"

"Yes, suh. I sung . . . I sung the songs to the kids. . . ."

"Of course." I supposed she meant hymns. "Would you pray to God right now? Pray to God to set you free? Pray to God to take you home?"

I waited several seconds, as she sobbed on wordlessly, then I implored: "Just in your mind, pray to God—He'll hear you." With increasing fervor, I pushed on. "Pray, and *believe*, that you can leave . . . that you can put this tragedy behind you, and not exist on this plane in fear."

"I can't leave the baby!" Clearly her devotion was boundless.

"The baby has already gone on," I said.

"No, suh. I hear him crying."

Ah, a wedge at last! "You do? You hear the baby crying? But you told me the baby is dead."

"Yes, suh."

"So you're hearing the baby cry . . . from where? From where his soul is now, aren't you?"

She didn't answer. Perhaps she was pondering my question.

"You can go to that baby," I said, "if you but will. Because that baby is with God. The baby in its own way is calling you to come to be with him and God. You can go, if you will but believe. Please pray to God to let you join Him and the baby . . . and to take you away from this, where you've allowed yourself to be trapped. You will find freedom. . . ."

At that moment, I sensed by the shift in Marianne's posture that Effie was finally leaving it, and I hastily uttered a parting benediction: "God is answering your prayer. Peace to you, Effie. We love you."

And she was gone.

Perhaps you can understand the sense of relief I felt when Marianne—and it was indeed Marianne, herself—finally returned to consciousness, glanced around, and asked what happened. With tears on her face and muscles fatigued by prolonged sobbing and emotional tension, she knew the session hadn't been tranquil.

I looked away from her face for the first time, to see most of the group standing in a circle about us. The lone exception was Phil Fairhill, who was looking on from the only doorway to the room. His towering figure practically filled the opening. We were to learn the significance of his determined stance later.

As we did for the Angelica experience, we gathered afterward to review the episode and to psychically seek more information about Effie and the circumstances of the predicament in which we found her. We still didn't know, for instance, whether Effie actually had met her end at the hands of her mistress, as she feared, or in some accidental way.

First, Marianne related her impressions. "Effie was a very, very unhappy, cold energy," she said. "You could feel it in the room the minute you walked in. The place just simply radiated fear and unhappiness and anxiety. It didn't feel threatening; it didn't feel angry, but very, very unhappy and very frightened.

"This time I went in [to trance] with the understanding that yes, I would probably lose some time in the process, and this time it was of my own [conscious] choice and volition that I sat down and allowed this energy to enter me—with a certain amount of trepidation. It felt so very unhappy, and yet I felt a very strong need to contact whoever it was in the room that was experiencing so much misery for such a long, long period of time.

"Coming out [of trance], again there was this feeling of being just absolutely emotionally drained—again, the stiff muscle feeling. I guess the first thing I was aware of was Phil's rather massive bulk blocking the doorway. I was also aware from the expressions on the faces of the people around me that whatever had happened apparently had been emotionally very moving. Again, I have no conscious memory of what was going on, so my retrospect is not as good as from those who saw it firsthand—'cause I wasn't there!"

After this report, both Marianne and Sandie Fairhill went into psychic trance to explore the circumstances via their Higher Selves. Here, in part paraphrased, are the principal points emerging from that exploration:

> Effie was pacing, waiting for her mistress to get back, Sandie reported in trance. When she heard the door open downstairs, as the mistress returned, Effie got even more [rattled and distraught] and started to run down the stairs to beg forgiveness, even before the mistress discovered the baby's death. In her hysteria, she slipped on the stairs and fell, breaking her neck.

With this revelation, we understood why Phil had stood so resolutely in the doorway: he intuitively had blocked it against any attempt by the distraught Effie to bolt again for the stairs, this time in Marianne's body. He explained it later: "When Effie came through Marianne, I suddenly sensed that she [Effie] had died by a fall, possibly from the window behind her, but most likely on the stairs. Since Effie now was in control of Marianne's voice, at least, I intentionally blocked the door so she couldn't get to the stairway, if she suddenly exercised physical control as well."

While Marianne has never had a ghost usurp total bodily control—and Effie gave no hint of doing so—Phil's action struck us as prudent, nevertheless.

The story continued to unfold from Sandie's lips: Effie, in her mid-teens at the time, was not a slave; she was the daughter of a family freed before or at the outset of the Civil War. She, and her mother before her, had loyally served the family of the baby's mother even after receiving their freedom.

The baby was born in the late 1860s. It was not the first child, two girls having been born earlier, while two other children had died. The parents, greatly wanting a son, were highly thrilled by the boy's birth. But he was birth-damaged and ill with jaundice. His attending doctor did not expect him to live, but Effie, very attached to the baby, wasn't told of this. She only knew the baby was sick and that she had instructions from the doctor for his treatment. But she was ignorant of how serious his condition was. This was intended to spare her worry over him and to keep her at ease in caring for him.

But the parents knew the child would never survive childhood—very likely not even to his first birthday (which he didn't; he was just months-old at his death). His mother had gone out, leaving him in Effie's care, as was her usual charge. When he died, Effie—in her ignorance of his precarious state of health—feared she was somehow at fault, and would surely be held responsible by the family. We know the results. Had Effie known, she would not have reacted so tragically, and fatally, as she did.

We feel that relief of Effie's spirit indeed was achieved during this session, although the long history of the house suggests there may be other (presumably benign) entities attached to it. Janet's husband, intrigued by the episode, later checked various official records in an effort to authenticate the existence of Effie and the family she served. However, the old town's records are incomplete for the Civil War era, with the years between 1843 and 1875 missing completely. In the limited time he spent, he did find some county records of names and dates of events that seem to fit, but which fall far short of concretely confirming the information we received and will not be detailed here. As later chapters will confirm, hard proof of a ghost's presumed mortal lifetime is often tantalizingly elusive. Nevertheless, Janet came to feel Effie did once live—and came to her untimely end—in their house.

Like Angelica, Effie remained earthbound only because, in her obsession, she didn't know she had already died. In Effie's case, though, it was an unawareness, during her *life*, of the baby's true condition that contributed to her tragedy.

Apparently it's over now, though. When, a few weeks later, we asked whether the room's atmosphere had improved, Janet happily reported that she no longer felt uncomfortable, even after prolonged activities in the room of former gloom, and that she no longer had the feeling of something behind her on the stairs. She had moved her son into it with absolutely no qualms.

We like to feel we had a role in Effie's finally finding peace. This episode still ranks among the most moving of our ghost encounters and was a landmark early step in our growth and understanding.

4

CHARITY ENDS AT HOME

Our local Metaphysical Research Group meets monthly, usually with a guest speaker to discuss one or another of the multitude of topics lumped under the term "metaphysics." At one meeting in 1985, Connecticut psychic Roger Pile, who was spending the summer in Richmond, was our featured speaker. He was experienced in ghost encounters, having interacted with them for years via the mediumship of his former wife; as noted in Chapter 1, he considered "soul rescues" of unaware ghosts to be one of his life's missions.

Roger had promised for this meeting a demonstration of his rescue technique. Marianne and I, with our then very limited rescue experience, were eager to learn from this seasoned "rescuer," and we attended in a state of anticipation.

Some wondered if the demonstration would succeed, since the modern clubhouse site of our meeting had no known history of hauntings. Perhaps there were no ghosts lurking about there. However, Roger assured us that, while most ghosts seem to be associated with a specific location or person, "place" is a physical property of reality; in nonphysical realms, place only defines where a being's attention is focused. Thus, it isn't necessary for a medium to be physically at a "haunted" location; he or she can reach out psychically to it. There was no reason why we couldn't "raise" a ghost from anywhere.

Roger asked Marianne if she would serve as medium, and she, assenting, proceeded to slip almost immediately into trance. In just moments, I saw in her the now-familiar signs of an emerging external presence.

Before we could address it, the ghost suddenly blurted, "I am *not* leaving this house!" The voice was strong and defiant.

I was Marianne's usual questioner during mediumship, so Roger signaled me to respond. I said, "Good evening. Would you like to identify yourself?"

"Who are you?" the ghost barked.

"I am the husband of the channel you are using at the moment," I replied, mirroring the ghost's testy tone. It wasn't yet clear whether the visitor was male or female.

"I don't know what you're talking about!" Well, of course. A ghost oblivious to its death wouldn't grasp what was happening or know who we were.

This one clearly was belligerent. I decided to step aside and let Roger cope with it. "I would like to defer to you, the expert," I said to him.

"I'm not an expert," he demurred; then, to the entranced Marianne, "But I'll be glad to talk with you. What is your name? I need to have a name to talk to you by."

"MacKenzie, sir!"

"Ah, MacKenzie. That's a fine Scotch name," Roger said, a Scottish burr sneaking momentarily into his voice.

"Charity Scott MacKenzie," she elaborated quickly, settling the question of gender. Interestingly, she did not have an accent typical of a southern woman of the time.

"Charity Scott MacKenzie." Roger rolled it off his tongue. "Tell me, Charity, where do you live? Where are you?"

"On Franklin Street." Franklin is a principal street in the heart of Richmond (and several miles from the apartment where we were).

"Can you tell me what year it is?" Roger asked her.

After a long pause, she replied, "Don't you know?"

"No, I'm afraid not," Roger said, in a befuddled tone. "I'm getting old—my brain's getting rattled—perhaps you can help me?"

"It's 1865, sir," she told him.

It was educational for us to watch this experienced "rescuer's" technique for drawing information directly from the emerging personality. Marianne and I sought to uncover details missing from our direct interchanges through Higher-Self psychic inquiry, but here we saw how Roger—through expressing abysmal ignorance and sympathetic concern—managed to glean many details right from the "ghost's mouth."

"1865! Oh, dear," Roger sympathized. "That must be a *terrible* year for you, is it not?"

"There've been several very bad years, sir."

"And what is—there's something terrible happening, I think," Roger fished. "Now, can you tell me what is going on? I hear *terrible* things are going on."

Charity seemed to consider her answer. "I don't know. I sent Elizabeth down . . . they were going to go by Libby prison and check and see if they could find out what's going on. We saw flames from the window."

"Oh, dear. Flames! Is there a fire, or—or what is going on? I'm terribly confused," Roger said.

"I don't know." The belligerence was gone from her voice.

"You don't know," Roger echoed. "I understand there's a hostility, is there? There are soldiers?"

"Hostilities? What a way to put it!" Charity retorted. "Yes, there are soldiers."

"What kind of soldiers? Can you tell me?"

"Both my husband and my son were soldiers, sir." Her voice was tinged with both lament and pride.

Roger apparently missed her use of the past tense. "Oh," he said, "and where are they soldiers, if I may ask?"

"They're dead!"

"Oh, I'm sorry." Roger's sympathy sounded heartfelt.

"My husband died here," she continued, "but he died of wounds received . . ." She stopped in mid-sentence for several moments, then continued, "my son died at Shiloh."

"I see. And were they soldiers of . . . ?" Roger probed. "Again, I—I'm terribly confused."

"The Confederate States of America," Charity said, flatly.

"I see. . . . Well, I'm sure they died very, very honorably, ma'am. . . . Now, can you tell me, what is the last thing that you remember?"

"I had Elizabeth going out of the house to go down and see what was happening. . . ." She suddenly turned defensive: "I'm not leaving this house, sir! It's all I have!"

"It's not necessary," Roger assured her. "It's not necessary, and I'm here to help you."

"How . . ." she began, but Roger pressed on.

"Relax," he said, softly, "feel—feel that I am here to help you. I am your friend, ma'am."

Charity began to weep. "I've given enough to this God-forsaken war . . . it's taken my husband, it's taken my son. . . ." She broke off in uncontrollable sobs.

Suddenly, a new voice intruded: "Mama?" Unnoticed by the rest, Sandie Fairhill of our group had slipped into mediumistic trance. Evidently Charity's daughter had dropped in from whatever is her present realm to help us.

Charity didn't hear the newcomer through her gulping sobs. "It's all right . . . it is all right," Roger soothed, trying to quiet her so she could hear her daughter.

"Mama, it's over," the new voice said, very softly.

"It is OK," Roger continued to soothe. "It is fine. We're here to help you . . . we're here to help you resolve all of this."

"Mama, it's over," her daughter said again. "It's done."

Finally, Charity heard. "I don't understand, Elizabeth," she said hysterically. "What's done?"

Roger explained softly, "The war's over."

"It's been over for a long time, Mama," Elizabeth confirmed, meaning, of course, for more than a century.

Charity didn't grasp that significance. "Oh, Elizabeth, we knew that when Petersburg fell," she sobbed.

"Mama, time—much time has gone by since the war has been over. The war has been over for years and years. It's time for you to let go. . . ."

"I don't think the moon is full, Elizabeth, but you're talking like you have a touch of lunacy," Charity declared. "What do you mean?"

"Elizabeth," Roger interposed, "Perhaps I can talk to your mother—if I may. . . . I will try to explain to your mother."

He returned to Charity. "Charity, listen to me," he said in a near-whisper. "It's all right. Now listen to me: Charity, you are . . . you are dead! OK? It's all right, yet you are alive. We are here to help you go to Heaven. Would you like to do that?"

Gasping, she said, "Are you telling me, sir, that you're here to kill me?" Her voice rose in a crescendo of alarm: "I'm a defenseless woman—this house is all I have—what do you mean I'm dead?"

"Charity, I want you to *think*," he replied, "think back—and I have to take you back. . . ."

"Carter's—" she began. Her Husband? Or son?

"What is the last thing you remember?" Roger pressed.

"I told you, sir, I remember Elizabeth going down to Libby prison to see what the news was."

"OK, and then the next thing . . . what happened after that?" he asked.

Charity took a reflective pause, then said, "Smoke."

"Yes—OK, smoke. Where was the smoke coming from?" When she remained silent, he said, "It's all right; we are here. You are safe. . . . Remember that. You *are* safe." When she continued in silence, Roger repeated, "Where is the smoke coming from?"

"Front parlor," she finally spoke. "I thought one of the darkies possibly had let the chimney clog."

"That's right," he agreed. "And then what did you see?"

After another long pause, she again said, "Smoke."

"That smoke . . . a lot of smoke," Roger ventured. "Did it not engulf you? Did you not choke?"

"I don't know. I don't know." She was blocking the memory.

"You must look at yourself," he insisted. She sobbed in stress, and Roger tried again to put her at peace: "It's all right, we are here."

"If Edward and Carter were here, you wouldn't be talking to me like this," Charity retorted.

"No, I'm talking to you [like this] because we're friends. We're here to help you."

Her voice was a whisper. "I don't understand. Who are you?"

"It's all right, it's all right. . . ." Roger purred. "Look upon yourself. See yourself what happened. You must understand what happened. . . . And that's OK."

She didn't respond. "It's all right," he repeated. "This is to help *you*." After a long silence, he continued. "You are seeing yourself, are you not? And you are understanding what is happening. . . . You are in a house on fire—and that is all right. Feel . . . you have warmth and love surrounding you; it's all right. But you must see what's happened. And understand what's happened—and it's all right."

Suddenly, Charity yelped in astonishment: "Edward!"

"Yes, he is coming for you!" Roger exulted. "Are you ready to go with him?"

She only gasped in recognition and sobbed in belated understanding. "Go with him in peace and love and joy," Roger said, in blessing, while the rest of us joined in.

With a final sigh, Charity was gone.

"Thank *you*, Elizabeth," I offered, as she, too, withdrew.

This episode was a milestone in Roger Pile's considerable experience, for he never before had seen or done a "rescue" in which a second medium spontaneously channeled a deceased loved one of the ghost, as Sandie did here, to penetrate the troubled soul's fixation and entreat it to move on. Some aspects of this case were incorporated by Roger, now a Ph.D., into his doctoral dissertation.

This supportive channeling of a ghost's loved one was a first for us, as well, although Marianne and Sandie had earlier used a simultaneous trance technique in psychic research. We asked Sandie what induced her to join in the session in this way. She revealed that she intentionally relaxed to a point of incipient trance at the beginning of the session, making herself accessible as a channel for any energies intent upon helping the "earthbound" personality. "I became aware of an outside energy anxious to participate—so anxious that it seemed to push me aside. So I simply let it through," she explained. It's a method we've used again in later rescue episodes.

This episode also presented some new elements to Marianne. "What was different about Charity," she later related, "was that I wound up working with an 'interviewer' other than Bob, as I discovered after coming out of trance. Too, [because of the unrelated location] I wasn't aware of any energies floating around the clubhouse, so it was somewhat like having an open house for whatever 'spook' was floating around with the greatest need for release. So I assume this was something agreed on earlier by my SC and Charity's.

"Charity was not as hard on the body as Angelica and Effie. Maybe it's because my body is becoming accustomed to being a welcome wagon for traveling ectoplasm shows, but I wasn't as exhausted by Charity as by the other two. Compared to Effie, she was nothing."

It was instructive, during this episode, to watch Roger's practiced technique for directly extracting information. Having no foreknowledge or known history of a "haunting," but simply taking "cold" whatever entity responded to our invitation, we started with no predefined inkling of the ghost's circumstances. Yet, thanks to Roger's adroit questioning, we obtained a fairly complete picture of a southern lady named Charity MacKenzie, who, in 1865, lived in a slave-staffed home on Richmond's Franklin Street and whose husband, Edward, and son, Carter, had both died as soldiers in the war—the latter at Shiloh. Her daughter, Elizabeth, though out on an errand to nearby Libby prison, presumably lived in the home with her. We also learned that Charity died from smoke inhalation in her home.

According to history, it was in the early morning hours of April 3, 1865, several days following the fall of Petersburg, that two massive explosions shook Richmond. Confederate forces, preparing to abandon the city to approaching Union forces, had blown up the central military powder and ammunition stores. Awakened citizens peering out their windows saw flames licking the sky in the initial stages of the intentional burning of the city by retreating forces. Before it was over, there would be more than 900 homes destroyed—some of them on Franklin Street. Presumably most residents had ample warning to evacuate; perhaps the MacKenzie residence was overlooked and Charity became an inadvertent victim.

It was with a feeling of relief and accomplishment that we could take part in assisting this proud and terrified lady to finally put the turmoil behind her and rejoin her loved ones.

In addition to learning from Roger, this episode also led to our education with respect to confirming a ghost's validity. One might suppose, as we did, that enough full names and locations emerged from this episode to be useful fodder for historical research. Given several MacKenzies—a couple of which were members of the Confederate forces—and a family residence on Franklin Street in Richmond in the 1860s, we should be able to find some validating references among various records of the time. Encouraged by this seeming wealth of specifics, and the local reverence for Civil War data, I began a search for historical confirmation of our ghost's mortal existence. It turned out to be harder than expected.

It shouldn't be surprising to learn that records from the Civil War years are spotty and incomplete. The last prewar Richmond city directory was published in 1860; the Richmond MacKenzies of any historical prominence died before the 1866 directory was created. (We don't know about Elizabeth. We don't know if her name was changed through marriage, or whether she survived the war.)

Unlike modern city directories, which often list all family members in a household, the early Richmond directories listed only heads of households, businesses, and employed individuals. The 1859 directory lists no MacKenzies. Neither does the 1860 issue. But it does include one spelled "McKenzie,"[1] first name not

1. Spelling is inconsistent. Historical references to the same individual variously spell it MacKenzie, Mackenzie, and McKenzie, and there's even an obscure Mackenzy. One author capitalizes it differently in separate books.

included, who was employed as an artist in water colors at an art or (possibly) photo gallery. This individual does not appear in the 1866 directory, which also has no MacKenzies.

The 1860 census, which also lists only heads of households and household members having a different surname, shows no MacKenzies or McKenzies in the Richmond area. From these references, one might conclude the MacKenzies never existed.

Yet other sources confirm that indeed there were MacKenzies in Richmond in years before the war, at least one of which was a person of some means. Highly regarded Richmond historian Mary Wingfield Scott says a William MacKenzie built four houses in Richmond, circa 1810–1820.[2] These were on Grace Street, one block north of Charity's Franklin Street. Scott says at least one was either burned or demolished in the 1850s.

This same William MacKenzie[3] is credited with building another house in 1814 on Richmond's Main Street at Seventh. Yet another building on Main Street (at Fifth) for many years housed Miss Jane MacKenzie's finishing school for females, before it was replaced by a mansion in 1847.

Whether this "Miss" Jane was the same Jane MacKenzie, widow of William, who bought eleven acres of his land when it was up for auction in 1829, isn't clear from this source. It was on this acreage that a mansion called Duncan Lodge was built on Richmond's Broad Street in 1843.[4]

From this, it's clear there were pre-war MacKenzie properties

2. Mary Wingfield Scott, *Old Richmond Neighborhoods* (Richmond: William Byrd Press, 1950). Reprinted 1975 by Valentine Museum, Richmond.

3. This William MacKenzie and his wife, Jane, were foster parents to Edgar Allan Poe's sister Rosalie. William MacKenzie presumably was related to the Jack MacKenzie that Poe himself counted among his old friends.

4. Mary Wingfield Scott, *Houses of Old Richmond* (Richmond: Valentine Museum, 1941).

all around Charity's home on Franklin Street. Main street is one block south of Franklin, Grace is one block north, and Broad, in the center city, is two blocks north. Yet no record can be found of a MacKenzie residence on Franklin itself. The city directories of the time did not cross-reference by street addresses, and insurance policy records—a useful source of historical information—list no MacKenzie properties insured in Richmond in the mid-1860s. Similarly, there are no real estate tax records of that time reflecting the MacKenzie name.

As for seeking Edward and/or Carter MacKenzie listed among the ranks of Confederate soldiers, fragmented military records of the era are widely scattered and not readily researched without more information as to company, regiment, etc.—a formidable task currently beyond our reach.

One item mentioned by Charity that history does confirm is Libby prison. There is no doubt it existed; in a warehouse, owned by someone named Enders but which had housed a business by a ships' chandler named Libby, it was the most central prison in the city.[5] It was on Canal Street, three blocks south of Franklin, just a short walk from Charity's house. It was likely the closest place for Elizabeth to find soldiers or other officials who might have knowledge of what was happening. Of course, the mere existence of Libby prison, though long since gone, in no way confirms Charity's tale.

This is one of those cases for which historical validation remains tantalizingly elusive. While research efforts have turned up no explicit records of the individuals represented here, they have shown how incomplete are the records of other MacKenzie individuals who we know existed. Such a lack of confirmation does not automatically imply invalidation of the related episode,

5. *Op. cit.* Scott, *Old Richmond Neighborhoods.*

but I must note that in light of subsequent experience, such elusiveness is characteristic of many ghost encounters. The issue of confirming ghosts' authenticity is addressed further in later chapters.

5

A Victim of Religious Dogma

In our early ghost encounters, such as that with Effie, we would first hear, from the residents of the "haunted" premises, the events leading them to suspect an entity. Then, following direct contact, we turned to Marianne and others' SC's to explain the underlying circumstances.

In later cases, particularly those where the afflicted residents felt that the "haunting" energies were highly troubled, we developed the practice of calling upon our respective SC's for information *before* attempting ghostly contact, seeking a preview of the hazards and challenges ahead. We did so for this episode, which differed from our earlier ones in that this ghost just repetitiously screamed "help." So the SC's were our *only* source of information.

Anita[1] came to us with stories of troublesome discarnate energies in her stylish south Richmond apartment. Having some psychic sensitivity herself, she consistently felt an uncomfortable, almost threatening energy in her bedroom. At least once, she had fleetingly glimpsed two figures, one of which she believed to

1. A pseudonym.

be female. Feeling their energies to be troubling and menacing, she asked our help in resolving the "haunting."

The team for this occasion consisted of Lou Ebersole, Charles Strickland, Marianne—psychics all—and myself. Upon touring the premises, Marianne perceived nebulous, shapeless auras of two discarnate entities, one of which she saw as red. In Marianne's aura "color code,"[2] red indicates some degree of mental derangement. From this, we inferred the possibility of facing an irrational being.

As she reported afterward, "In walking into Anita's apartment, [I sensed] the two dominant feelings were fear and rage. Having committed to trying to release these energies, I was willing to do it. Working with such close partners as Charles and Bob was reassuring; having walked into that room and felt what I did, I would not have been willing to work with anyone else. I needed to be working with very familiar, very trusted people in this instance, because it was a very scary situation."

Charles, in the meantime, was having visions of violence. It appeared intuitively to him that a man attired in garb typical of colonial days was attacking a female with an axe—certainly an instrument of terrifyingly violent execution. As he put it later, "The 'red' entity that Marianne sensed was a male figure; one I believe was a highly religious zealot who mistakenly thought his daughter had compromised her virtue, and what started out to be a severe beating turned in raging passion into a murder involving an axe.

"His energy was disturbing because he was 'religiously crazy.' He was *so* restrictive in what he would allow as acceptable behavior

2. Contrary to books that set forth a rigid, universal relationship between various aura colors and their meanings, each perceiver's "color code" is unique to that perceiver. Two perceivers viewing the same aura may agree on the traits it reveals, yet they individually may describe quite different colors.

—in his understanding of 'the word'—that his belief grew suffocating and he became [literally deranged]."

This intense scene played out in Charles's mind somewhat like the residual, repetitious apparitional "movie" hauntings mentioned in Chapter 1. He felt from the outset that the female was the object of our "rescue" mission.

After we familiarized ourselves with the premises and settled in for psychic adventure, Marianne relaxed and went into trance. I first sought an audience with her SC—who manifested as a male personality—to allay, or at least minimize, my apprehensions before inviting an external entity. What follows is the essence of my conversation with her SC:

Recognizing his emergence, I greeted him: "Hello?"

"I love a captive audience," he cracked.

"You love a captive audience? You have a rather tense audience tonight!"

"Yes, I know," he said. "We all are."

It surprised me that tension afflicted those functioning at cosmic levels. "You are, too?"

"Certainly. It's a highly energized situation we're in the middle of, and certainly, on the spiritual level, we're not immune to that kind of energy."

"Well, is it possible," I entreated, "now that we have you in our midst, for you to control what would come through when you step aside? . . . And before you do, I would like your suggestions on how to approach the unfortunate girl, if indeed that's what we're going to be confronted with."

"I don't mean to be sarcastic or flip about this," he remonstrated, "but if, from the spiritual standpoint, we had a good way of approaching the unfortunate girl, she would have been gone two hundred years ago."

"I was hoping you would have some feel for what might reach

her," I persisted, "if we are able to communicate with her verbally."

"OK, there has been an almost continuous attempt to get her to see the light, and to follow the light. It's around her, it's waiting. . . . What you're going to be going through is a wall of terror, more than anything else. And if she can just simply be redirected to—to look to the light, which she should perceive as a very, very clear and intense blue. . . ."

"A clear and intense blue," I repeated to confirm. "All right."

"That's her own Superconscious trying to pull her in," Marianne's SC explained.

"Can you give us some information? What was her age?"

"Her age was fifteen," he said. "Her name was Eliza."

I wanted to be sure I could communicate with her: "She does speak English?"

"Yes, indeed. Uh, as Charles was being informed by [his SC], she was the daughter of a household where the father was a fundamentalist religious zealot. He suspected she had been keeping company with a neighbor's son; the neighbor's son was not of the same faith, and the father had made up in his own mind that she had been sexually permissive, which she had not been, and [with his axe] he was simply removing this abomination from the eyes of the Lord."

"Well, if the perception here of a red aura is correct," I observed, "he was a little unbalanced himself; am I correct?"

"Yes."

I wanted reassurance that, should we get into a tight situation, we could terminate it without resolution, if necessary. "Can you give us some guarantee," I asked, "of putting a time limit on this, if we are unsuccessful. . . . Can you eject the other [from Marianne's self] and return [yourself]?"

"Yes," he assured. "With the support that I've got around me right now, yes, I certainly should be able to ... but I would certainly second the suggestion by [Charles's SC] that the double pyramid [protective energy] formation will be nice so far as the energy flow goes."

The "double pyramid" he referred to is a supportive "safety shield" concept originated by Charles. It's a tenet of faith that we are never challenged by psychic energies capable of overpowering our own Superconscious resources;[3] however, adding some conscious-level protective imagery at least bolsters our sense of security, and perhaps does genuinely add to our armor by concentrating a reservoir of positive psychic energy. It certainly can do no harm.

Here's Charles's technique: because we would be exposing Marianne, as medium, to possibly violent and irrational energies, Charles sat to one side, facing her; similarly, Lou sat at her other side, also facing her. Both envisioned projecting and focusing protective psychic or cosmic energy to Marianne in an expanding cone, thus centering her in the "double pyramid" where the bases of the cones joined. While this precaution may be fanciful, it seems to work—even if only by enhancing the medium's confidence. Lou and Charles had taken their positions even as Marianne's SC was speaking.

Lou spoke up: "[The double pyramid's] in place now, sir."

"I'm aware of it."

3. This tenet of faith applies personally to we who were directly involved in this episode, but I can't say with assurance that it extends to everyone. Certain rare cases of apparent uninvited possession by *something* malevolent, after intense investigation by the Roman Catholic Church, are deemed genuine. Some individuals may indeed be susceptible to some degree or another of forcible entry and manipulation by malevolent or even simply opportunistic incorporeal entities. This is why we admonish novices and others to be wary of "opening" themselves to unknown influences via the Ouija board and other incautious experiments.

Lou seized the moment to ask, "One question: is the perception that once the girl's gone, the other [personality] will go, too—is that correct?"

"Yes—the other one actually has gone; what you've got here is one of these situations where the spirit of the girl is here, but it's one of these 'time warp' circumstances that takes place at the site of a violent incident like this." That explained Charles's perception of a ghostly tableau.

"This is the 'movie film' kind of haunting?" I asked.

"The movie film, right. He immediately took his own life, after killing her."

"Ah! And has moved on?"

"And has moved on."

So, I concluded, the "movie" haunting simply is residue in time-space from an emotionally intense event, an insentient psychic pattern. "Then we really shouldn't fear his . . ."

"No, but that violent energy is still there."

"I see," I said, for expedience, although I really didn't. Even though insentient, does the pattern retain the strong, negative psychic energy that created it? Apparently so.

Anita, the resident, asked if that was the energy she'd been feeling.

"Yes," came the answer, "very much so."

"Will that dissipate if we can [release the girl]. . . . ?" I asked.

"It should . . . but no guarantees! But it should."

"OK," I said, pressing to get to the heart of our mission. "We have survived terrified young ladies before; maybe we can do it again."

"OK," Marianne's SC conceded. "It will be good rehearsal for what's to come later—not here,"[4] he hastened to add.

---

4. We now know her SC was alluding to the yet-to-come "rescue" of three serial-killer victims described in Chapter 13.

"Thank you," I said with some relief. Her SC withdrew, opening Marianne's "channel" for the ghost to manifest.

Just twelve seconds later, a piercing, repetitive scream suddenly filled the room.

Trying to penetrate it, I repeatedly shouted "Eliza! . . . It's all right!"

I went unheard. Punctuated by gasps for breath and my shouts, the wailing scream continued for forty-five seconds. That's a long time to hear anyone scream; when it's one's wife, it seems an eternity. Not that Marianne was consciously suffering; I knew she was out of it, not knowing that her voice was straining with Eliza's abject terror in the face of instant, violent death. Yet it was unnerving to me.

Finally, the screaming trailed into gasping yelps of "HELP! HELP!"

"Eliza," I said during a pause in her breathing, "It's all right."

"HELP!"

"It's all right. . . ."

"Help!" Her pitch was dropping.

There were several more of her yelps and my unheard assurances. Then I interjected, "Eliza . . . Eliza, it's over. It's over, you're among friends, and you're all right." Then again, in a whisper, "You're all right."

She still wasn't listening. "Listen to me," I demanded. "We're here to help. We're helping . . . if you'll only listen, we will help you."

She continued wailing and sobbing, and I repeated, "If you will listen, we will help. . . . It doesn't hurt anymore. . . . It's all over, it's all over."

She was gasping for breath. "You're with friends," I assured her. "Breathe deeply and relax. It's all over, and you are with friends."

She quieted, Marianne's body still panting from the screaming. I said, "Hello, Eliza."

After several moments of silence, I repeated it. "Hello. . . ."

Then she smiled. This could only mean she was finally seeing the light. "You're smiling!" I said. "Can you speak?"

Without answering, she yelped with that note of surprise that comes from being suddenly and unexpectedly drawn to a higher realm. "Ah, it's over," I exulted. "It's so nice it's over!"

Continued heavy breathing. Was she still here after all? "Hello?" I probed again, anxiously, but she was gone. It was Marianne who answered, to my great relief.

Marianne described her experience later. "My big fear was being aware of both a very frightened entity and an insane energy," she said. "I didn't want the insane energy to come through me. I had to put a lot of faith in [my SC] that it would be the frightened one, not the maniac, who came through. Indeed, that was the way it turned out.

"Again, I was aware of the sensation of having been physically drained; I had very, very tight muscles. I think her fear must have translated strongly to my body muscles—I think I ached for a day or two afterward."

Excepting a few "Helps" and yelps from Eliza, our encounter with her wasn't a conversation; it was a monologue. Yet it's our perception that, by bringing Eliza into the physical plane and repeatedly reassuring and calming her, we did break through the barrier of terror that frustrated her own Higher Self and any other nonphysical personalities in their attempts to get her attention.

We don't know who Eliza finally saw; it may have been her own enveloping SC personified. We made no postepisode queries. Whatever or whoever it was, she found release. Her smile was the clue; no one still terrified by what is perceived as impending certain death by the blow of an axe could possibly sport a smile.

6

CHILDREN FOR A CENTURY

When Jim, a longtime friend of Marianne's, heard of our early experiences with ghosts, he revealed that he and his wife, Cheryl, suspected a discarnate presence in their home. They sometimes heard noises, he said, usually at night and seemingly from the attic; when they would investigate, they'd find no conventional explanation. As Cheryl told us, "It doesn't do anything destructive; it just walks around and makes noise."

So it developed that just months after our Angelica baptism, we were climbing the stairs to the attic of Jim and Cheryl's comfortable home in northern Virginia. Emerging to find only standing room and flooring, and having wrestled over much of my life manhandling assorted articles in and out of various unfinished attics, I mumbled appreciatively, "This is the way an attic ought to be." Well, almost. It was unheated and bore a November chill.

While I disgressed, Marianne focused on our objective. She peered quickly about. "Yes. There's something up here," she said, matter-of-factly. "But no heat!"

We quickly retreated to the warmth below, where Marianne elaborated. "Your ghost is female," she announced.

"It is?" Cheryl seemed surprised. "How can you tell?"

Even though Marianne sometimes does not perceive the auras of "earthbound" souls, she did this time. Not a distinct figure, just a shapeless, hazy ovoid. "Up there in a far corner, there's a rose pink aura—which I've never seen associated with a male. It's a color I usually connect with a young—or very naive— female.

"And," she added, "the aura's clear, so I don't think it's a particularly troubled soul." Having contended with Angelica's highly distraught state, I found this comforting. Perhaps this ghost would be easier to deal with.

Jim needed to verify his understanding: "I take it, from what you say, you think there is one [discarnate] here. . . ."

"Oh, yes. For sure, there's *something* up there." She repeated her perception that it was a young female.

After some idle speculation over the nature and history of this entity, we decided to go to the source. It was time for Marianne to go into trance and invite the ghost to speak through her. She sat on a couch, closed her eyes, and began her trance-inducing relaxation routine.

On the tape, there was only the whirr of the hot air furnace for the several moments it took Marianne to "go under." Jim and Cheryl watched in silence, not knowing what weirdness to expect. Then Marianne's voice spoke—not as a ghost, but in the tones of her own Higher, Superconscious self, familiar to me.

For Jim and Cheryl's benefit, her SC spent several minutes discussing various kinds of discarnate entities in general. He touched on concepts of free will, reincarnation, karma, and Spirit realms—concepts ranging beyond our scope here. To the point, however, was the observation that the entity, whose name we were told was Melinda, and who had died at the age of eight in a carriage accident, now had no immediate need to move on; that she had known Cheryl as Rose in a previous lifetime, was attached to Jim[1] (through events in allegedly previous incarnations of both), and that we should not discourage her presence.

So perhaps this wasn't to be a "rescue" of an "earthbound" soul, after all. Still, having come this far, we all wanted to hear from the ghost. I asked Marianne's SC to step aside and invite Melinda to speak through her.

There was another long silence. Then Marianne's hands began moving up and down her arms, touching, caressing, as Melinda's essence renewed the tactile experience of being physical.

I spoke to her: "It feels strange to be back in physical form, doesn't it?"

"Yes." It was almost a whimper, this first childlike sound.

"Hello, Melinda," I said gently.

"Who's that, Papa?" she asked. We took the "Papa" to be addressed to Jim, that being consistent with the past life information Marianne's SC gave us.

"I'm just a friend," I explained.

I must not have convinced her. "I'm scared," she said in a whisper.

I tried to soothe her fear. "You're among friends. There's nothing to be scared of. This is a chance for you to [directly] enjoy some loving relationships."

Recalling we were told that Melinda knew Cheryl in another lifetime as Rose, I ventured, "Perhaps Rose would speak to you."

Cheryl picked up the cue. "Hello, Melinda," she said softly.

"Hello. . . ." It came in a faltering whisper.

"Do you think of her [Cheryl/Rose] as Mama?" I asked. "And Jim as Daddy—or is it Papa?"

"Papa."

---

1. Which explains why Jim also had noticed some manifestations, while single and living in another location. Some ghosts are attached to locations; others are attached to persons.

"Are you pleased that they now know you are with them?"

"Uh-huh." I took that to mean yes.

Seeking to draw her out, I asked, "Is there something you would like to say to them?"

"Hunh-uh." Beyond a doubt, this was a no. Her reticence boggled me.

As I pondered my next question, she abruptly said, "I'm scared. I'm going back!"

And she did.

Which shows that, while ghosts may scare some people, people may scare some ghosts.

This was one of our shorter direct conversations with a ghost. Afterward, Marianne shared some of her perception of it: "Initially, I was self-conscious [about going into trance] because I had not done this kind of thing in front of Jim, who I've known since high school.

"I gather Melinda was an aware Spirit. I had no problem at all working with her energy in my body; it was relatively comfortable and very, very gentle to work with.[2] I think because Melinda was aware, I had some vague consciousness of what was going on during the trance, unlike my experiences with unaware entities."

We never firmly determined whether Melinda remained here by choice, or only because she feared moving on; since we were told that "rescue" was inappropriate in this instance, we were content to leave her as we found her—a reclusive eight year old going on a hundred.

In contrast to the reticent Melinda, Alice was a talkative and assertive child ghost, and clearly ignorant of her death. We met

2. As later experiences were to show, Marianne finds children's energies usually very easy to work with, because they're generally very trusting and happy to have a means of expression after years of silence.

her during the summer Roger Pile, the researcher and teacher of metaphysics from Connecticut, was visiting Virginia.

Roger accompanied us on a trip to Oakley, an estate in Central Virginia, where our group sometimes gathered. Once owned by a medical doctor who conducted his practice in a dedicated building on the premises, Oakley's atmosphere was subtly uplifting to our spirits. Its caretaker at the time was a member of our group, giving us access to it for our occasional social outings.

You'll recall from Chapter 4 that Roger was experienced in ghost encounters, having interacted with them for years via mediumship by his former wife; in fact, he considered "rescues" one of his life's missions. Thus, it wasn't hard to prod him into doing another rescue for those of us gathered there at Oakley. He was willing; would Marianne be the medium? She would.

We were seated in the main house at Oakley. Roger was confident that a ghost would come forth there, and Marianne was game to try. As she put it afterward, "Since Alice was not on-site, but was a 'remote' release, I was not aware beforehand of any particular energy, except for the usual ones that float around Oakley. The environment at Oakley is always warm, always friendly, so it was a very easy place in which to do this. I tend to be very attuned to what the atmosphere is in the room, house, or location where I'm channeling, and at Oakley it always felt safe. Enough so that I had no reservations about working with Roger Pile [instead of Bob]."

Marianne began her self-induction into trance, and we waited expectantly and a little apprehensively. In due time, she showed the physical signs typical of entry by a foreign consciousness. A ghost was present.

"Yes?" Roger prompted.

"If you're another doctor, I'm not going to take anything else!" The words from Marianne's lips clearly were those of a young girl—a very determined young girl.

"Well . . .," Roger began, but she cut him off.

"It tastes nasty. [And] I'm not going to be stuck again. . . ."

Hastening to reassure her, Roger said, "No, I'm here to help you. Now, I really need to know your name. May I have your name, please?"

"Alice," she said, matter-of-factly.

"Alice," Roger repeated, his voice reflecting approval of the name. "How old are you, Alice?"

"I'm almost seven," she said proudly.

To build rapport, Roger bordered on patronizing her: "Oh, that's a big girl. You're really getting to be a big girl, aren't you?" He pressed on. "Now, what is this nasty medicine you're taking? Did they tell you what it was?"

"It's for the in-flu-enza." She separated the syllables as a child does when learning a difficult word.

"I see. That—that probably tastes pretty nasty. Is it castor oil?"

"I don't know. It just tastes nasty!"

"Boy," Roger sympathized, "when a medicine tastes nasty, it's YUCK!"

Alice rolled on. "Gerald brought the in-flu-enza back from France," she announced.

"Yes, [I see]," Roger agreed. "Do you know what year it is, Alice?"

"I'm going to be seven in three months. . . . So's Alexandra. She's my twin."

Roger gave perfunctory acknowledgement of this revelation: "Oh, that's nice. Did they tell you what year it is? Is it 1910? 1914?"

"I don't know. I think it's Wednesday."

"Well, it could be." (Actually, it was Saturday.) Giving up on a literal date, Roger mounted a roundabout attack: "Does your father have a car?"

"A *what?*"

"OK, does he have a horse and carriage?"

"Yes."

"Do you know what a car is?" Roger persisted. "Have you seen a car—an automobile?"

"I don't know." Clearly, cars were unknown to Alice.

"That's OK," Roger comforted. "I was just trying to find out about when it is ... but that's all right." Changing tack again, he asked, "Now, you have influenza, do you, Alice?"

"Yes."

"I bet it makes you feel terrible, doesn't it?" Roger's tone was syrupy-sympathetic.

"It makes my tummy hurt so bad. It makes me hot all over—but it doesn't anymore!"

This could be an opening for explaining to Alice that she was no longer physical. "No, of course not ...," Roger began.

Unheeding, she pressed on: "But they make me stay in this room all by myself."

"They told you to stay there, didn't they?"

"Yes," she said, dolefully.

Roger finally got his opening. "But you don't have to stay there anymore, Alice—did you know that?"

"I'm not going anywhere without Alexandra," Alice retorted, "and they won't even let her come in to see me! Ever since Gerald got back from France and had the in-flu-enza."

"Well, I know," he said, "but, you see, the reason your tummy doesn't hurt anymore is because you ... you no longer are in your body. Did you know that? That's why it doesn't hurt anymore."

But Alice was riding her own train of thought. "Miz' Smithson said he got the in-flu-enza fighting the Huns."

Roger feigned wonderment: "He did?"

"Yes. She said if he hadn't messed with the foreigners, he

wouldn't have brought it back." Alice's voice reflected Miz' Smithson's indignation.

"Well, yeah, that happens, sometimes," he concurred. "But—uh, we have to help *you*. And this . . ."

She cut him off again. "It doesn't hurt anymore, so you don't have to give me anything else," she said, defensively.

"Oh, I'm not going to give you any medicine," Roger assured her, "because any medicine I could give you now wouldn't work."

Alice changed the subject. "It gets lonely up here. Do you have any children I can play with?"

"Well," he offered, "I can take you to somewhere that you would have children to play with. . . ."

"I'm not going without Alexandra!" She was adamant about that. "We do everything together. We sometimes change clothes, and sometimes we even can fool Miz' Smithson."

"You can!" More mock amazement. Then, clearly not yet having found the magic lure, Roger pushed on. "Where do you live," he asked Alice. "Do you know the city you live in?"

"Yes. . . . It's the country place. Mama and Papa stay up in Alexandria [Virginia], but we stay in the country place."

"Oh, I see," said Roger, as though he actually did. Shifting again, he asked her, "Can you describe how your mother is dressed? What sort of dresses does she wear? What sort of dresses do *you* wear?"

"Well, we don't see our mother very often."

"Oh, is she maybe in Washington most of the time?"

"Yes."

Roger pursued this direction. "Does she visit . . . has she gone to the presidential balls? Has she ever mentioned seeing the president of the United States? Did she ever mention that?"

"Is that a Mister Wilson?" Alice asked.

"It could be." Making an assumption, Roger ventured, "Yes, Mister Wilson is definitely president of the United States."

"My daddy says there's a Mister Wilson who's an idiot."

Roger, being agreeable, but careless in his time tenses, said, "Well, a lot of people thought Mister Wilson was an idiot. That's all right. Uh. . . ."

Alice abruptly reverted to her own predicament: "They won't even let Button, the dog, come up. Button made a puddle on the rug in the nursery, and Daddy called him a 'misbegotten mongrel'—and Miz' Smithson says I'm not supposed to say 'misbegotten.'"

"Probably not," Roger agreed, chuckling along with the rest of us.

"There are lots of 'misbegottens' in the Bible," Alice proclaimed, in defense.

This triggered a side comment by Roger that he thought the Biblical word was "begotten," not "misbegotten." When asked if she concurred, Alice simply commented, "I don't know—I'm not supposed to say it!"

Laughing at this, Roger steered the conversation back to the issue at hand. "Well, Alice," he said, "I want to help you . . . and I have to tell you that where you are, there are no children, and there probably won't be any children. But I can help you to where children are, and—I think, also—would you like to see your mother?"

"I want to see Alexandra!" Alice insisted.

Roger sounded dubious. "Well, I'm not sure I can do that, but I can try. I can try to bring Alexandra to you. If . . . if Alexandra came, would you go with her?"

"Go where?"

"Well, to the place where children are," he temporized, "where you can have fun and play . . . and really enjoy yourself much better than where you are now."

"Can Button go, too?"

"Yes, Button can go too."

"No rugs?" she asked.

"There are no rug—" he began, then, "Button won't do anything on the rug, where you're going. Because Button's a good dog." He was on a roll, now. "Button didn't like your father calling him a misbegotten mutt. . . ."

"Mongrel," Alice corrected.

Accepting her rebuke, Roger said, "Now, let me see if I can bring Alexandra in."

Suddenly and unexpectedly, a new voice burst forth. It came from the lips of Sandie Fairhill, a medium and member of our group. "I'm here. I was just waiting for everybody to stop talking so I could."

"Well, welcome, Alexandra," Roger responded.

"She shows off like that," Alice declared.

Roger addressed Alexandra. "Would you be willing to take Alice across with you?"

"Oh, yes. We've been waiting for her for quite a long time."

"Thank you very much for coming," Roger said. Turning to Alice, he continued, "You see, Alexandra is here to take you across to that place where you can play with all the other children—and Button."

Alice was wary. "Where?" she demanded.

"Well, it's a place called Heaven," he explained. "Have you heard of Heaven?"

Her voice was tinged with suspicion. "It's where dead people go!"

It was time she faced the truth. "Well, Alice," Roger said gently, "you are dead."

"No, I'm not—the pain's stopped!"

"Of course," he pointed out, "because you are in Spirit. You are in Spirit, and Alexandra is here to show the way and take you with her. And that's all right—you see, most people don't realize they are Spirit. . . ."

"What's he talking about?" Alice demanded of Alexandra.

"Well, let me explain it to you this way," Alexandra said, in a tone of resignation. "Look down at yourself, right now."

Through Marianne's eyes, Alice looked down at Marianne's adult body. "It doesn't look like you remember yourself, does it?" Alexandra challenged.

"Unh-unh," Alice conceded.

"You're dead, kid!" Alexandra said, flippantly. "Come on. Momma and Poppa are waiting."

There was no defiance, no doubt left in Alice. "OK," she said flatly, and she was gone.

So ended what we deem a successful "rescue" of a child-soul who apparently succumbed to the influenza epidemic early this century and didn't realize she had died.[3] We don't know how—or when—Alexandra died; however, she no doubt was aware of it and moved on accordingly, coming back when she could speak to Alice with our help. It's our understanding there's always an entity available that an "earthbound" ghost will respond to, once the ghost's attention is directed away from its self-limiting obsession.

This was the second occasion, in Roger Pile's experience, when a second medium channeled a loved one of the ghost's to help convince it to move on; it was the first where the visiting loved one directly escorted the "rescued" soul to the next realm.

As for us, this was another lesson in the techniques of drawing information out of a manifesting personality. Without resorting

---

3. While unawareness of a surviving essence of its discarnate state often follows from sudden, unforeseen physical trauma, apparently it also can follow a less abrupt death from illness. It seems reasonable that a sick child may enter terminal delirium or coma in ignorance of the possibility of death and may die "unprepared." This could account for Alice's unawareness, as well as Molly's in the next chapter. An adult would likely be more aware of the possible consequences of serious illness, thereby being better prepared for the possible advent of death.

to psychic research, we can infer from Roger's guidance of the conversation that Alice lived in a Virginia country home, perhaps near Oakley, with her twin sister and a strict governess, that her parents were comfortably affluent and well-connected in government circles, that Gerald probably was a brother who served in France in World War I, and came home with the flu, and that Alice succumbed to the flu during Woodrow Wilson's presidency. And of course we mustn't overlook Button!

In these episodes we have seen how entities that died as children retain a child's consciousness to the present, even though they have existed on the earth plane since their deaths for as long as 70 years. (Wilson became president in 1913; we didn't establish the time of Melinda's physical life.) In general, it seems time stops for "earthbound," or "unaware" souls at the moment of death. A similar element of time stasis occurs in other cases in this book, as well. This supports an accepted metaphysical tenet which holds that time in nonphysical realms is, if not nonexistent, at least indeterminate.

7

AFRAID OF JESUS

When we first became involved with the "rescue" of "earth-bound" souls, it was by urging them to look to Heaven, or God, that I stumbled onto hooks that worked. I decided early on that this was a universal lure—at least to anyone having an expectation, or even a slender hope, of surviving physical death as an incorporeal being. But, as so often happens in exploring metaphysics, what at first seems a simple rule turns out to be less than universally applicable.

While knowing that Heaven might not be a compelling lure for some, it hadn't occurred to us it could be the very opposite—a highly undesirable destination in the view of a surviving soul. But it was, for Molly.

Bonnie, of our group, "volunteered" us to Larry,[1] a musician friend of hers who believed his apartment was haunted. There was the chill of winter in the air, as a handful of us converged on the timeworn apartment in what's called Richmond's Fan

---

1. "Larry," "Diane" and "Kay" are pseudonyms to preserve the participants' anonymity.

(because several streets diverge, fan-like). Entering, we exchanged introductions and pleasantries and shortly got down to work.

We listened to Larry and Diane, his live-in girlfriend, recount a number of incidents. Larry was troubled by untimely and inexplicable lamp failures, which seemed to him to relate somehow to his trips out of town. Even brand new bulbs expired—as many as eight or nine of them in recent months—and not when first turned on, as is the common bulb failure mode, but when someone would walk into the room where the lamp was on. While excessive lamp failures could possibly be nothing more than maladjusted power line voltage in the apartment's circuits, some of the couple's other experiences were suggestive of poltergeist activities.

There had been several occasions when they heard knocking on the walls and sounds like doors closing, when no one was near them, and Diane once saw one close by itself.

Diane's attention was further whetted by temporary disappearances of various common objects, such as a book or a decorative knickknack. As she put it, she would "turn the place upside down" searching for them; yet, though the apartment was too small to really misplace something in it, the missing objects were nowhere to be found, until they would turn up at some later time.

Occasionally, bottles and other items were knocked or pushed off shelves. Sometimes Diane just sensed a vague presence in an alcove—one with a seemingly gentle energy, just watching and listening.

Then there was the night when Diane and her friend Kay were there alone and, upon retiring, Diane wound her clock, checked the time, and set the alarm for 7:00 A.M. She was certain, because Kay subsequently had asked if she set the alarm and she had rechecked it, then moved the clock away so she couldn't reach out and turn it off in her sleep.

She awoke later to see the clock reading 8:45. But the alarm hadn't gone off at 7:00, and it was still dark outside, so she knew something was amiss. Getting up and checking the kitchen clock revealed that it actually was only 2:15 A.M., and when she examined her alarm clock, she found the alarm now was set for 9:00!

Diane satisfied herself that Kay had not entered her room at any time during the night; she herself had slept soundly; yet the clock time was advanced by nearly five hours and the alarm setting changed by two—both of which she and Kay had double-checked for correct settings upon retiring. Diane was convinced that something paranormal had happened that night.

After we heard their stories, Marianne went into her familiar trance-entry routine. In a few moments, her hands began the telltale caressing of her limbs that betokens the emergence of a long-discarnate entity, renewing the tactile sensations of physicality. I offered my usual commentary: "It is a strange sensation to be physical again, isn't it?"

"Can I come out now?" a small, childish voice asked through Marianne's lips.

"Yes. . . . Would you—can you tell me who you are? What is your name?"

"Molly," she said, without hesitation.

She sounded very young. "How old are you, Molly" I asked.

"Seven."

"Do you live here?"

Another example of a ghost taking a question in its narrowest, most literal sense. I meant the building, or that neighborhood; she took me to mean the room she asked to come out of. "Sister Agnes Xavier sent me up here to the pentence room."

I was puzzled. "To the repentance room?" I ventured.

She corrected me: "Pentence!" I later concluded she had meant "penitence."

Moving on, I dropped into a Roger Pile ignorance mode. "Uh, you'll have to excuse me, Molly. . . . I'm going to have to ask a lot of questions, because I'm just kind of a stranger here, and I don't know much about it." To confirm the seemingly obvious, I asked, "Who is Sister . . . ? Is she a Catholic lady? A nun?"

"Yes."

I guessed, "Are you in an orphanage? A Catholic orphanage?" Nodding, she said, "This is the school."

"This is the school? And you are seven years old? Molly," I pressed on, "do you have any idea what year this is?"

"February . . .," she hazarded.

"February of what year?"

She seemed uncertain. I tried prompting. "Could you remember . . . it was New Year's not very long ago—what was the new year?"

"Ninety-three," she responded.

"1893," I concluded, aloud. Now, to find out what happened then. "Molly," I began gently, "something happened when you were sent up here . . . something that you can't remember. . . ."

"I 'member," she retorted.

"Oh, you can? Do you want to talk about it? Or is it too hard to talk about?"

"Sister Agnes," she wailed, "said I was very, very wicked. She said Jesus the Savior made my tummy hurt so bad. She said it wouldn't have hurt if I hadn't been a very wicked girl."

Oh-oh! This was going to be touchy. Sister Agnes certainly had spoken imprudently, yet I dared not disparage her; clearly Molly shared the traditional Catholic veneration for nuns and priests. I couldn't undermine that trust.

I chose my words as carefully as ad-libbing permitted: "Well, let me tell you something. Sister Agnes, I believe, meant well— but Sister Agnes was . . . was mistaken. Do you believe that Sister Agnes could be mistaken?"

"No. . . . It hurts so bad!" she whimpered. "I said the Pater

Nosters over and over ... must have been a hundred-zillion-million times. . . ."

So she didn't believe Sister Agnes could be mistaken. This certainly was going to challenge my powers of persuasion. "Let me tell you something, Molly," I explained, "Jesus was not making your tummy hurt."

"Sister said He was!"

"Jesus is very forgiving . . .," I insisted, "and Jesus will even forgive Sister for being mistaken. . . . But something happened to you, and you really shouldn't be here anymore; you should go home—and home, Molly, for you now is to be with Jesus—"

"NO!" Molly yelped, in terror. "He made my tummy hurt!"

Her abject fear took me aback. Despite what the Sister had told her, it just hadn't occurred to me that the child could truly fear Jesus. "No," I hastened to assure her, "He didn't. . . ."

"He punished me," she insisted.

"This is where you are ... mistaken." I argued, "Somebody has misled you."

"No!"

"Yes, Molly . . .," I began.

"I like it *here!*" Molly was adamant.

"But," I countered, "there are other things for you to do, and there are loved ones ... there are loved ones for you to join." Seeking the magic "hook," I asked, "Why are you an orphan? Were your parents killed? Do you know?"

"Sister Agnes said that my mother was a 'fallen woman.' And she died when I was born because Jesus our Savior punished her, too. . . . I don't wanta' go there."

Sister Agnes certainly had indoctrinated this child with her own severe judgment values. How could I, a total stranger, convincingly override what this authority figure had told her? "Do you know that your mother loved you?" I suggested. "And do you know that your mother would like to have you with her right now . . . and you can be with her. . . ."

"She was a bad lady!"

"No, she was not a bad lady," I argued, "and her sins have been forgiven, whatever they were. That's what Jesus does."

"No." She remained unbelieving.

"Yes, Molly," I insisted. "Jesus forgives."

"No. He made me hurt. . . . I didn't do anything," she sobbed.

This poor child's needless anguish tore at my heart. "Jesus didn't make you hurt. Some bad disease [I guessed] made you hurt; it was not Jesus."

"The people here are nice," she pleaded, "I don't wanta' go."

"The people here can't help you anymore, Molly," I explained, "but your mother, and Jesus, would like you to join them—and *everything's* forgiven . . . and you *could;* all you have to do is believe."

I gambled that she might perceive her mother calling to her: "Listen! Now listen, carefully. Listen . . . do you hear your mother calling, Molly? Listen carefully. . . . She's calling you from Heaven. You know where Heaven is."

"Where they make people hurt," she responded.

"No, no, no!" I exclaimed, aghast. "Unh-unh. People hurt here on Earth. People don't hurt in Heaven, Molly. Believe me; I'm your friend. . . . All I want is for you to be happy and for you to rejoin [those who love you]. Because you're out of place here now.

"Things are different here," I continued. "Would you—just for me, Molly—just pray to God? Pray to God and say, 'Please take me home, where I can be loved.'"

She merely shook her head in denial. There was a long pause, while I pondered my next appeal.

"You're closing your eyes to the greatest love in the world, Molly," I gently chided.

"He made me hurt. He made my mommy die," she wailed.

"No, no, no!" I whispered. "That is wrong . . . and you must get that out of your mind. Things here on Earth caused that—and you can get away from all of that, simply by *thinking* you can. Open your mind. Pray. You know how to pray."

Groping feverishly in my mind, I grabbed at another possibility: if she feared Jesus, perhaps as a Catholic, she would seek solace in Mary. "How about praying, maybe, to the Virgin Mary?" I ventured. "Did she ever do anything wrong to you? Don't you think the Virgin Mary loves *all* children? Including you?"

Molly was silent. Maybe she was considering what I was saying, so I continued. "Don't you think the Virgin Mary would be glad to have you with her?"

"Sister says I'm wicked . . . that nobody loves me." Presumably, not even Mary.

I suppressed my rising rancor over the nun's intimidation of the child. "You listen," I admonished Molly. "Listen. Somebody is calling, Molly. Somebody is saying, 'Molly, you're not wicked. Molly, we love you. Molly, come home to us!' Listen carefully—you'll hear it."

Suddenly came the sound of a strange voice: "Molly!" Unexpected, it was channeled by Charles Strickland.

I had no idea who was manifesting. "Yes?" I queried.

"This is Father Stephen," he proclaimed, in measured, sonorous tones.

Ah! A breakthrough. At last, someone she had known.

She made no response. "Are you listening, Molly?" I prompted. "Please continue, Father."

"Your stomach hurts because Sister Agnes struck you, as you know," Father Stephen responded. "It is not the will of Jesus, of course. . . . It is time for you to come with us, now."

"No. You'll hurt me," Molly cried.

"You know Sister did not mean to hurt you, and she is sorry," the priest intoned. "Will you join us now, Molly?"

Tearfully, she asked, "Will you hurt me, Father?"

"No, you know I would not."

"Will Jesus hurt me?"

"Never at all, Molly. Jesus is love, as you have been taught."

Molly finally seemed to bend a bit: "Can I have a puppy?" she asked.

"You can have *two* puppies, if you wish," Father Stephen assured her. "And we'll feed them together, as we did the other one in the garden."

"Where are we going?"

"We are going home."

Molly wasn't fully sold yet. "This is home," she argued.

"Home is with Jesus," the priest countered.

"He won't hurt me?" she asked, anxiously.

We all joined in a chorus of "No's." Father Stephen confirmed it: "No, He is quite incapable of hurting you—as am I. And Sister Agnes. It was not intentional."

There was a long pause, while Molly seemed to weigh her decision. "Go, Molly!" I encouraged.

"Come with me now, my dear," Father Stephen implored. "Come, my child."

Then I sensed her essence departing from Marianne. "Goodbye, and God bless you," I bade her. "And thank you, Father."

Then he was gone, too.

This episode, like every ghost "rescue," was unique. It's the only one in our experience, thus far, in which the subject had an abject fear of Jesus, which certainly made the prospect of going to Heaven a threat instead of a promise. Seeking an alternative, I had supposed that surely one reared in a Catholic institution would be receptive to the embrace of the Virgin Mary—but Molly wasn't. Molly being orphaned, the mother she'd never known wasn't an inducement, either. Finding the "hook" that works is a different challenge in each instance.

Marianne later commented:

> Molly was scared. There was a lot of mixed emotion in that apartment. I picked up on Molly's fear and unhappiness, and on the repressed anger that seemed to pervade the environment she died in. It was with some trepidation that I invited this energy in.
>
> "I guess I'm probably most nervous going into a trance state and inviting a discarnate energy, when I'm aware of either anger or rage being present. I would not want to channel somebody who was eaten up with anger or rage. Confusion, fright, I can deal with, but anger and rage, no. And I wasn't exactly sure what I was going to get with Molly.
>
> As it turned out, hers was a very loving child energy, which, as I have said, does not take much toll on the body. Not unpleasant at all. What made this a unique experience for me was that this was the first ghost release where I worked in [trance] in tandem with Charles, when he allowed Father Stephen to speak through. But again, this is all retrospective, because I don't remember what happened.

In common with all these episodes, it was the subject's perception of a loved or revered one's having called or come to lead the subject away from this plane that finally achieved success. We are deeply thankful for, and were quite surprised by, the emergence of Father Stephen. Thankful because he led Molly home, and surprised because, as Marianne commented, this was the first time Charles channeled an external entity.

When later we asked Charles how he happened to be drawn to channel Father Stephen, he was at first at a loss as to how to explain it. Like Sandie in other episodes, Charles had entered the session not only to observe, but to cooperate in any way circumstances may dictate. He simply lost consciousness and became an available channel when the deceased Father Stephen came to dispel Molly's fears.

Though Charles had channeled his own Higher Self on previous occasions, channeling another's disembodied personality was a new experience for him. Upon reflection, he reported little recollection of the priest's words, but, he said, "I recall a very warm, caring, loving feeling; just a genuine affection embracing all people—and of course poor Molly in particular." The feeling persisted long after Father Stephen had left with his charge.

Fundamentally, this case resembled all others in the sense that its very uniqueness made it a learning experience for us. For instance, while this was our second experience in which a young child with a fatal illness remained unaware of her physical death, she differed from Alice. Alice had moved just far enough past death to say, "It doesn't hurt anymore," but Molly was still focused on the pain in her last hours of life. Alice had a complete and affluent family, in contrast to Molly's orphaned state. Alice had a twin who finally led her home, while Molly had no beloved family members from her lifetime. Little of what we learned with Alice was directly applicable to our experience with Molly. Because each experience was unique, each brought new challenges and new knowledge. That's probably endless; since no two persons are alike, it follows that no two ghosts are alike, and neither are their "rescues."

The dialog with Molly left some troubling loose ends. In particular, Father Stephen implied that a blow from Sister Agnes was the prime cause of Molly's abdominal pain and, by inference, her ultimate death. But it's hard to suppose that even a rigidly judgmental and righteously punitive nun, however misguided, would strike a child a mortal blow.

To explore this troubling aspect, we asked Marianne to engage her Superconscious source to psychically fill in some details. Here are some that came to light from that session:

There once was a school for an orphanage on the site (but not the present building).

The year was in the 1700s, not 1800s, as I had thought (Molly only said "ninety-three"; I had assumed the century).

Molly's mother, also named Molly, had originally immigrated as an indentured servant. She became pregnant aboard ship and actually delivered at this site, then a mission of what Marianne's SC referred to as the "Sisters of Mercy."

Sister Agnes, attending to the birth, even then was unduly judgmental, and she neglectfully allowed the elder Molly to die of bleeding due to delivery—a crime of omission, not commission.

As for the key issue here, Marianne's SC reported:

> Younger Molly, in the process of being punished, was kicked in what was an inflamed appendix. She actually died of peritonitis. Sister Agnes interpreted this as God's punishment of the child. She probably was of the belief that if the mother was a sinner, the child was also going to be a sinner; the fact that both of them had red hair built this into her mind.

The role of Father Stephen, according to Marianne's SC:

> Father Stephen was the priest attached to the mission at that point and had developed quite a fondness and affection

for young Molly. As he noted, they had found a stray cur out behind the mission, and together they had been sneaking food out to it. Father Stephen knew that he'd be in trouble with the Sisters for giving food to an animal at a point when they were heavily involved in charity work and could not see the sense in diverting scarce food to an animal. But the child and the priest had developed a close friendship.

We were surprised to learn from Marianne's SC that the ghost of Molly's mother also remained about the site, but did so by choice and was not an unaware soul. We were equally surprised to hear that Sister Agnes also remained on this level. Regarding Agnes, he said:

> That's a very angry energy that's still here [centered in another apartment in the same building]. She started out feeling well-motivated in life and ended up being generally despised by all of the nuns who were working with her. She carried self-righteousness to an extreme. [She remains here] mostly due to anger; she comes and goes intermittently. She's held here to some degree by a tremendous feeling of guilt over Molly's death; she was aware of the [role of] the blow she'd given her. Possibly with young Molly gone, she may be willing to release and move on.

A side issue of curiosity: if the elder Molly and Sister Agnes, who must have shared a mutual animosity, frequented the same site, I wondered, how did they avoid some form of conflict or confrontation? Marianne's SC explained. "It's a little bit like two cats [that can't stand each other] coexisting in the same household—they're both very, very good at pretending the other doesn't exist."

And finally, we learned the poltergeist-like events Larry and Diane experienced weren't the young Molly's handiwork at all; they were caused by her mother, the discarnate elder Molly, trying to gain the mortal residents' attention. She succeeded, eventually leading to the release portrayed here.

There is little in this episode explicit enough to explore historically. A Father Stephen, a Sister Agnes, and two wards named Molly, all without last names, aren't likely to be found in sketchy records of the late 1700s. However, it seemed that a potential lead might lie in the channeled reference to Sisters of Mercy.

According to Richmond historian, Mary Wingfield Scott, a Father Timothy O'Brien established the Sisters of Charity (not Mercy) in a former Catholic chapel in Richmond in 1832. It wasn't until 1840 that a girls' school, and still later an orphanage, was added to this, which became known as St. Joseph's. (St. Joseph's Orphan Academy was still listed in the 1866 Richmond city directory, said to be under the charge of the Sisters of Charity.)

If the 1793 dating of the Molly episode is correct, however, it clearly predates the establishment of St. Joseph's. Another girls' orphanage was the Female Humane Society, which Scott says was founded in 1807—again, too late for Molly. We don't know who operated this one.

We have found one historical reference to the Sisters of Mercy in Richmond: historian Alfred Hoyt Bill, discussing the overburdened hospitals in Richmond during the Civil War years, notes in passing that "The Sisters of Charity and Mercy conducted the de Sales Hospital on Brooke Avenue." Whether this reflects two

2. Mary Wingfield Scott, *Old Richmond Neighborhoods* (Richmond: William Byrd Press, 1950, Valentine Museum, 1975).

3. Alfred Hoyt Bill, *The Beleaguered City* (Westport, Connecticut: Greenwood Press, 1946 and 1980).

separate Sisterly orders, or is the full name of one customarily shortened to "Sisters of Charity" isn't clear from this.

It seems reasonable, though, to presume there were two separate orders cooperating in hospital service. Other sources allude to distinct orders in the South during that era: Some of the Sisters of Charity from a convent in Emmitsburg, Maryland, began work at Harpers Ferry in June of 1861 (nearly thirty years after Father O'Brien's installation of the Sisters of Charity in Richmond) and served in other Confederate cities, specifically including Richmond, during the Civil War years. They further note that the Sisters of Mercy, from the mother house in Baltimore, served a number of southern cities during the war. Richmond isn't specifically mentioned in this connection; however, it being near Baltimore, the Sisters of Mercy well may have served in Richmond and been the latter half of Bill's "Sisters of Charity and Mercy."

All these references, though, belong to a time seventy years or more after Molly. In fact, later research eliminates the Baltimore Provincialate as a source of the Sisters of Mercy in 1793. According to the Sisters of Mercy Archivist, Irene Callahan, Baltimore Regional Community, this order of the Sisters of Mercy was founded in Dublin in 1831 and did not come to America until a few years later. Doubtless, it is to these whom historian Bill refers.

On the other hand, "mercy" is such a basic attribute of Roman Catholic Sisterhood nurses that, supposing our information is valid, there could have been other groups formally or informally known as the Sisters of Mercy, one of which Molly could have been a ward. Or conversely, Marianne's SC may have been in

4. Francis Butler Simpkins, and James Welch Patton, *Women of the Confederacy* (Richmond and New York: Garrett & Massie, 1936). The authors also note that Charleston (South Carolina) hospitals were served by yet another order: The Sisters of Our Lady Of Mercy, and Kentucky cities were served by The Sisters of Charity of Nazareth.

error on the date he seemed so confident of; nonphysical sources often have difficulty with physical-level time references. However, lacking sufficient details for more intensive research, we must add Molly to the ranks of ghosts whose presumed earlier mortality falls short of historical confirmation.

8

SHANGHAIED IN LIFE, TRAPPED IN DEATH

Richmond's Metropolitan Astrological Research Society[1] (MARS) regularly stages a "Festival of the Stars." A number of booths, or tables, are set up in a convenient location for the public to obtain astrological charts, interpretations, and astrological or psychic readings. These MARS fund-raisers are usually well attended.

In 1986, MARS held its "Festival of the Stars" in Richmond's old Main Street railroad station, in what was the heart of the city during the Civil War years and early in this century. Long since abandoned by the railroads, the building was lately converted into a hub of boutique shops.

Some of our sensitive friends who participated in the MARS festival told us they found the old station psychically uncomfortable, as though the location harbored some number of troubled discarnates. The sensations were vague, without detail, but discomforting. Not surprisingly, someone suggested we might be interested in doing some ghost research.

1. Since renamed the Metaphysical Astrological Research Society.

Sometimes a challenge offered is a challenge cautiously entertained. If there were numerous troubled souls centered in one location, what are the risks? Will they all try to manifest at once and overwhelm the medium? Will they line up and require individual "releasing" in succession? Will one act as spokesman and, if he's shown the light, can he induce the others to accompany him to it en masse? We had no answers.

The obvious way to find out is to try it. Not, in this case, by going physically to the location, but by "remote control," much as we did with Charity. For this exercise, we felt probing remotely might allow Marianne some selective control in contacting a receptive soul, while avoiding the psychic babble from others concentrated in the old station.

So Marianne and I went one evening to Lou Ebersole's apartment to face this new challenge. I had some qualms, to be sure. However, it is our understanding that mediumship occurs only with the consent of the medium's Higher Self, which always polices the actions of "outside" entities it allows to channel. Thus far, we've had no direct experiences contradicting this concept, though we also invoke various conscious-level safeguards for whatever protection they may add. As Marianne entered trance, I spoke first with her Superconscious personality. I asked him to allow but one soul through at a time, and to keep things within bounds for Marianne.

He gave his assurance, and retreated to make room for an external entity. After a period of silence, Marianne shuddered and began the now-familiar moving of hands over her arms and body, signifying that a foreign energy was exploring its newfound physicality. "Hello," I greeted. "It's been a long time, hasn't it?"

"Gawd! Now wot?" It sounded like we had conjured up an Englishman, cockney accent and all.

"Now wot?" I mirrored. "An opportunity to talk to someone who wants to be your friend. . . ."

"Who in bloody 'ell are you?" he interrupted.

"I am a friend of yours."

"I have no friends in this Gawdforsaken country!"

"Ah," I said, "may I ask what is your native country?"

"England, sir." He pronounced it *sehr*.

"England? Very well." I dropped into a Roger Pile role of apologetically humble ignorance: "Would you . . . you'll have to excuse me, but I'm a bit ignorant of the situation here. I'm sort of a newcomer to all this, and I have to ask some questions I hope you'll be kind enough to answer. First, would you tell me your name?"

"Jymes," he replied.

"And your last name?"

"Digby," he said.

Parroting his cockney, I said, " 'Jymes' Digby. OK, James. Thank you. I appreciate your cooperation."

He resumed running Marianne's hands over her arms and torso.[2] By way of keeping the dialog open, I observed, "The feelings you're getting don't feel like the body that you once were familiar with—but go ahead and enjoy the sensation of physicality, because *I* know, even though you don't understand, at this point, that you haven't been in this particular state for quite a while."

He made no response, so I resumed prying for information: "Uh, could I ask you, what year this is? You see, I'm *really* confused!"

"Coo! They was right," he snapped. "This country *is* full of ignoramuses!"

I certainly must have seemed so to him. I stuck to my quest.

---

2. We've thus far not ascertained whether an external entity entering a body of the opposite sex—such as the male James in Marianne's—instantly senses the unfamiliar gender without literally having to see or feel the obvious physical differences.

"Ah, yes, I will admit to being an ignoramus," I said with my best self-deprecating humility, "and therefore I must ask you to . . . to help me, in my ignorance. What year is it, James?"

"1775."[3] His tone was patronizing.

"Ah! When the Colonies were considering independence, I believe. Is that correct?"[4]

He responded obliquely. "I didn't ask for no part in this bloody fracas over here."

"How did you get here? Are you a member of His Majesty's service, in some way?"

"Not willingly, sir," he retorted.

"Not willingly? So you are. . . ."

"I was walkin' down Magdalen Street, mindin' me own bloody business and, next thing I know, I'm in the bloody British Army."

"Aha!" I exclaimed. "What we sometimes call 'shanghaied' . . . I'm not sure that's a term you're familiar with. So you are in the British . . . Army, did you say?"[5]

"Yessir."

"Do you have a rank? What is your rank in the British Army?"

Marianne's SC had indicated we might contact an entity with

3. If Digby was in fact in Richmond, there's a time discrepancy here. According to historians, Richmond first received prisoners of war in February 1776. As proposed later, it's possible, of course, that Digby—wounded and incarcerated—lost track of the passing days.

4. My error. James probably hadn't heard in 1775 that the colonies were seeking independence. While armed skirmishes in Lexington and Concord between patriots and British marked the opening of hostilities in April 1775, the colonists were first fighting for their rights as colonial Englishmen. In May, the Second Continental Congress elected to raise a Colonial army, with Washington as Commander in Chief. Of course, the formal Declaration of Independence wasn't adopted until 1776.

5. I have since learned that in his time, unwary men were kidnapped by "press gangs" and impressed into unwilling military service.

leadership experience. Evidently he erred, for James reported, "I don't have no bloody rank; I'm a foot soldier."

"A foot soldier," I affirmed. "Uh, where are you now, geographically?"

James's voice rose an octave in indignation. "How in bloody 'ell would I know? Oddly enough," he added, sarcastically, "they didn't discuss the itinerary with us."

"Kept you in the dark, did they? Isn't that just like the army?" I continued, commiserating with him. "Do you know, armies have been like that ever since there've been armies? The top brass think they know it all, while the poor people down at the bottom, who have to do the work, and do the fighting. . . ."

He interrupted impatiently. "Listen, myte, it wasn't *our* army that was the problem."

"Oh? Then whose army?"

"The bleedin' Colonials," he responded.

"Oh, let me see . . . are you a prisoner of the Colonials, now?"

His manner turned diffident. "I s'pose. . . ."

I pressed for details: "Are you, at this particular moment, incarcerated? Are you in a prison? A compound?"

"We was marchin' in to tyke Williamsburg,[6] and I caught a bloody musket ball in my side. . . . Damn' bleedin' Colonial leech was s'posed to've been pulling it out; next thing I know, I'm in this here classy warehouse,[7] supposedly waiting for the resolution

---

6. Williamsburg was the capital of Virginia in 1775. However, while Lord Dunmore, the British Governor, abandoned Williamsburg to patriot hands in July 1775, apparently the British made no effort to retake it, until they occupied it in April of 1781.

However, there was a raid on the Williamsburg powder magazine in 1775; this is discussed later in this chapter.

7. It's interesting that James dubbed his accommodations a "warehouse." In 1775, the town of Richmond, with a population of about 600—and not yet Virginia's capital—was a trading center for tobacco, furs, and other commodities

of this fracas, to be sent 'ome. That's all I want, is to be sent
'ome."

"A very reasonable desire that is," I agreed. "I have to sympa-
thize with you. However," I pushed, "there are some factors here
that you don't know, and I want to make you aware of them
because we're in a kind of strange situation here. It's simply this:
that you have, in fact, succumbed to your wound."

"Do you mind!" Finding this preposterous, James was irate.

I got a bit contentious, myself. "Yes, I mind. You have succumbed to your wound, and you really do not belong . . ."

"Gawd Almighty!" James was beside himself. "Of all the
leeches I could possibly get in this Gawdforsaken country, I get
one who's touched in the upper works!"

"Oh, yes, touched in the upper works . . . but in a strange way,
because if you will simply listen and consider what I have to say,
you may find it will be very liberating to you, and get you out of
this—this 'bloody, Godforsaken country'—because all you have
to do, sir, is to realize that you are free to leave."

James was speechless for the moment, and I took advantage
of the opening: "You are no longer bound to this physical reality,
because, sir, in point of fact, the year now is well past 1775. And
you have kept yourself—because of the fact that you don't realize
what has happened to you—you've kept yourself in this suspended
state of animation for—would you believe—two centuries?"

"No."

"No?" He seemed intractable on this point. Clearly, a change

---

and was formerly known as Byrd's Warehouse.

Apparently, there was only a two-cell county jail and no hospital in Richmond
in 1775. However, there were at least five "tobacco inspection warehouses" in
the heart of Richmond, some of which were within three blocks of the present
Main Street station, the presumed locale of the discarnate Digby and his fellow
souls. Perhaps he really was in a warehouse.

in tactics was in order. "I would challenge you, sir, just challenge you . . ." I started, then hesitated. "But before I do, I would like to ask about those around you: are there a number of compatriots with you, in the same situation?"

"Oh, yes. They have stacked us up."

An interesting expression; I wondered what he meant. "They have 'stacked you up'? Like—uh—cattle? Like livestock? Or like cordwood? How have you been 'stacked up'?"

This got me nowhere. "We've just been piled in here," he droned.

I dropped the metaphor and searched for his status among those with him: "Do you occupy, at this point, a bit of respect and leadership among a good many of your fellow prisoners?"

"Yeah, I s'pose. . . ."

"If you were to show them something that might get them out of the situation you're in, would most of them follow you?"

"Guv'nor, if I handed them the line you've been handing me, they would kill me!"

Since he didn't know he was dead, he failed to see the humor of his words. "Uh, that would be impossible," I observed drily. "Bear in mind the 'line' I gave you, sir. . . ."

"There 'e goes again. . . ." James interrupted.

"You have already departed your mortal form. . . ."

"Right!" James's tone dripped with sarcasm and contempt.

"But you have not departed this level—this earthbound plane of existence." I was on a roll now and would not be deterred. "You are existing here when you *do not have to,* and I'm going to suggest to you, sir, just as a challenge: I will *dare* you to honestly open your mind—to open your eyesight, your spiritual eyesight, to Heaven and beyond, and to seek—if you have any concept of God, any concept of something beyond mortality, something beyond lying in a hospital wounded or lying in a prison compound—to look, to seek, and to say, 'Take me home. I'm free.' All you have to do is *think* it."

"Coo-ee! Isn't that pretty!" James mocked.

"Isn't it! I'm challenging you to test it."

"I don't take no challenges from no damned Colonials," he retorted.

"Oh, did I say I was a Colonial? I don't remember having said that. You're jumping to conclusions, aren't you, sir? Just as you're jumping to conclusions about my being, uh, a little bit daft . . . a bit absent upstairs."

This seemed to give James pause. "If you ain't no Colonial, what are you?"

Since he already thought me crazy, I chose to go all the way. I spoke softly and earnestly: "I am a friend, coming back to you from another time, inviting you to free yourself from your self-imposed imprisonment by simply seeing—wishing—imagining—envisioning—praying, if you would like, to God."

"Gawd never done nothin' for me!"

"Aha! Well, maybe you might give Him a chance." At least James hadn't yet turned me off completely. "This might be a time when He can do something for you, if you would open yourself up to Him, and say, 'God, I'm willing to listen to you. Take me out of this; make me free. And bring my friends with me'."

For the first time, James sounded tired. "Myte, I just wanta' go 'ome. I don't wanta' listen to your blarney."

Perhaps he was opening another door for me. If God wouldn't entice him, maybe home would. "Where's home?" I asked.

"London," he mumbled.

"London?" I stalled.

"Yessir."

"Your home, sir," I countered, "is much higher. At this point your home is . . . Heaven, with God." James remained strangely silent, so I prodded a bit. "I'm sorry that you won't rise to my challenge, because you might be very pleasantly surprised—and you certainly have nothing to lose. . . ."

"Me old dad owns the Swan," James mused, aloud.

Intrigued by this turn, I asked, "The Swan? A pub?"

"Pub?" James seemed puzzled. "He owns an inn."

"OK. . . . Tell us about it. Where is it?"

"S'near the Northern Gate. . . . Me girl Meg works there. She ain't much on no fidelity, but a body would still like to know. . . ."

"OK," I suggested, "Maybe—*maybe*—if you would listen, you could hear Meg calling to you from where she is now. And maybe, if you heard her call, and you just, out of sheer imagination, said, 'Hey, I'm coming to you, Meg'. . . ."

"I've heard Meg call me many times," he announced.

"You have? But you haven't believed that it was Meg, have you? You thought it was your imagination."

"Delirium!" he corrected.

"Delirium, nonsense!" I retorted. "When Meg calls you, you answer. Respond, and you may be reunited with Meg in the blink of an eye. Take it from somebody who's daft upstairs. Give it a . . ."

"You are that!"

"I don't deny that," I continued the role. "But you have nothing to lose by trying, do you?"

"Yes, but I've heard her before," he demurred.

"But you've never before said, 'I hear you, Meg, and I'm coming,' " I countered.

Groping for excuses, James said, "An' everyone else would think I was daft."

I persisted. "You've never done it, have you?"

"No."

"You're *afraid* to!" I challenged, hoping he would rise to it.

"I ain't afraid o' nothin'—you can go to Beelzebub and give 'im my regards!"

Misunderstanding, I argued, "No, you're not going to Beelzebub. . . ."

"No, *you* are!"

"I may," I freely conceded, "but that's my problem, not yours. Yours right now is getting back with Meg—getting out of this situation. . . . And you *can*, if you only wish yourself to do it. *See* yourself doing it. Visualize it, consider it *possible.*"

There was a long pause. I hoped James was finally unbending a bit from his stubborn stance. "Do you hear Meg?" I asked.

But he still was smarting from my earlier challenge. "Jymes Digby ain't afraid o' nothin'!"

"Do you hear Meg?" I persevered. While we weren't hearing her, I believed he could, if he focused on doing so.

"Yes."

"You're afraid to answer her," I taunted.

"Go to 'ell!"

I was relentless. "You're afraid to say . . ."

"GO TO 'ELL!" James literally screeched.

"You're afraid to say, 'Meg, I'm coming'—and picture yourself going."

"Everyone here would think I'm as daft as you are!"

This reminded me of his unaware companions. "Take them with you," I pleaded.

James reverted to contemptuous sarcasm: "Right!"

"Sure," I chided. "There are many of them willing; they're waiting for somebody to show them the way." He said nothing, so I continued, "Most of them have their own 'Meg,' their own lady friend, who's waiting for them somewhere. . . . Answer Meg!"

Resigned at last, James said, "Oh, all right."

"All right!" I exulted. "Say, 'Meg, I'm coming.'"

And he did. He actually said it: "Meg, I'm coming." In that instant, barking a yelp of surprise, he left.

"Godspeed," I whispered. "God be with you." At long last, it was over.

I'm always relieved when Marianne's own consciousness

returns to the fore. As usual, I sought confirmation when she opened her eyes: "You're Marianne, I hope?"

"Right," she chuckled.

"How much do you know of what went on?" I asked.

This time she hadn't been entirely out of it. "It was one of those things of being kind of 'aside' from it," she said. "I got a sense of a British character. That's all."

This one, like every new ghost encounter, enlarged our education. As Marianne recalled, "The James Digby experience was interesting because this was [my first] male ghost. I felt strange, first coming out of trance, as if the male somehow hadn't fit my body—and I think James was as uncomfortable with my body, as it was with him." This seems to differ from Marianne's channeling her own SC, who also is male but doesn't feel strange; evidently her SC only projects verbal control and does not actually intrude his energy into her body.

This one was obviously a challenging case. It illustrates well how one may run into many dead ends, while fishing for the one "hook" that the manifesting soul will respond to. As you saw, God and Heaven were futile inducements to James. It was his own reminiscing about " 'ome," leading to reflection about the Swan and yearning for Meg, that finally gave me a viable hook. Since I didn't initiate this avenue of inquiry, but merely picked up on James's lead, it may seem mere luck that Meg came up at all. It's our experience, though, that—if a "rescue" is intended by the Higher Consciousnesses involved—persistence in questioning will sooner or later bring forth a hook.[8]

---

8. This is in keeping with our understanding that communications sometimes occur on the superconscious level between ours and the SC's of obsessionally oblivious, "trapped" souls, subtly guiding us on some subliminal level.

Our lesson here is to focus on the entity's obsession. For Angelica, Effie, and Alice, the focus was on loved ones who—by our time—could safely be presumed to be in Heaven. Thus, God, Heaven, and loved ones residing there led to workable hooks. James, though, was most strongly focused on his old physical neighborhood. Meg wasn't his prime focus; he liked her and wanted to see her, but his principal obsession was centered on home in England. Had I grasped and acted on this at the outset, I'm confident this rescue would have been easier and quicker.

In checking James's story against the history books, several differences beg reconciliation. First is Digby's assertion that he was wounded while on a mission to "take" Williamsburg, then Virginia's capital, in 1775; yet there was no British attack on Williamsburg in that year.[9] The only historical reference to military action that year in Williamsburg concerns orders by Lord Dunmore himself, while still in power there—albeit precariously—for a British force to remove the powder stores in the Williamsburg magazine and spirit them off to the British Navy ship, *Magdalen*(!). (Presumably, he wanted to keep the powder out of the hands of the increasingly restive Colonial patriots.) Historian Virginius Dabney writes, "[Governor Dunmore] ordered British Sailors to seize the powder . . . and they carried off a wagonload."[10] But according to Ivor Noël Hume, the powder-raiding party was led by a Lieutenant Collins and a detachment of fifteen British *marines*, which he later referred to generically as "soldiers."[11] Apparently we're not clear today whether they

9. As mentioned before, Williamsburg was occupied by British forces in April 1781.

10. Virginius Dabney, *Virginius Dabney's Virginia*, (Chapel Hill: Algonquin Books, 1986).

11. Ivor Noël Hume, *1775, Another Part of the Field* (New York: Alfred A. Knopf, 1966).

were sailors, marines, or perhaps even, as James Digby described himself, "foot soldiers."

In any event, history records no gunfire during the magazine incident. Apparently the patriots caught wind of the raid just as the raiders were slipping away. *Collier's Encyclopedia* says this ". . . provoked the first armed resistance in Virginia,"[12] and Dabney says, "The [patriot] militia turned out, intent on marching to the palace and seizing the Governor."[13] But Dunmore managed to placate them and they retired without gunfire.

If accurate, these facts cast doubt on Williamsburg in 1775 being the catalyst for James Digby's predicament. First, the British raiders apparently were navy or marine forces, not "foot soldiers"; second, in the absence of gunfire, he couldn't have been shot there. Third, the raid occurred in April 1775, several months before, according to records, any prisoners of war were sequestered in Richmond, as noted below.

It's not beyond reason to consider, as an alternative, that he could have been wounded in the considerable action in 1775 centered on the Virginia Tidewater settlements of Norfolk, Hampton, Suffolk, and Great Bridge. While the British in these offensives never advanced close to Williamsburg, it's conceivable the troops were told, at the outset of their Tidewater action, that their ultimate target was the capital city; with no grasp of the vastness of the new world, Digby could have understood he was "marchin' in to tyke Williamsburg."

It's notable that, according to historians, the first prisoners of war to be quartered in Richmond arrived in February 1776.[14]

12. *Collier's Encyclopedia* (New York: Crowell-Collier Educational Corporation, 1967). Volume 23

13. *Op. Cit.*, *Virginius Dabney's Virginia*.

14. So far as can be determined. Because court records for Henrico County (whose jurisdiction included Richmond) before October 1781 were destroyed by

Historians Ward and Greer report that, "Numbering about twenty-five in all, the group included wounded soldiers of the Fourteenth Regiment, captured at Great Bridge in December [1775]; seamen deserters and. . . ."[15]

This suggests that perhaps Digby's "march to Williamsburg" actually ended at Great Bridge in the final weeks of 1775. This is consonant with prisoners arriving in Richmond early in 1776 (and Digby's overlooking the advent of the new year; when wounded and a prisoner, one readily may lose track of the days), as well as the number of compatriots he alluded to.

According to Ward and Greer, these prisoners were ". . . quartered in a house of Turner Southall, then county lieutenant of Henrico. . . . [They] were kept in Richmond until June 1776, and were then sent elsewhere."[16] There's no mention here of a "warehouse"; yet it seems unlikely that twenty-five prisoners were conveniently kept in a private home for four months.

They had to be kept and cared for somewhere; evidently the only prison facility in Richmond then was the Henrico County jail, with two very crowded cells. Too, as noted in an earlier footnote, there was no centralized hospital in Richmond then. It wasn't until 1872 that a smallpox epidemic led to the opening of a "pest house" on the John Cocke plantation, where Dr. William Foushee administered vaccinations. It seems within reason that one of the tobacco warehouses might well have accommodated some wounded prisoners.

In this instance we have a complete name, nationality, and alleged date. It's conceivable that British records of those unfortunates pressed into involuntary military service remain extant and

the British, we don't know if prisoners might have been processed through the local courts before that date.

15. Harry M. Ward and Harold E. Greer, Jr., *Richmond During the Revolution (1775–83)* (Charlottesville, Virginia: University Press of Virginia, 1977).

16. *Ibid.*

would reveal a James Digby shipped to the colonial front in those years; or perhaps U.S. records of British prisoners of war could be found containing his name. However, mounting a search for such records is beyond us, at present.

There is another unresolved issue in this case: did James's companion prisoners follow him out of bondage? Frankly, we don't know. By the time we finally got James sold on leaving, we had had our fill, and, to date, we've not explored this issue further. We'd like to think he swept them along with him.

9

SIMON SAYS, BUT CHILD OF THE MOON DOES NOT

Among our newer acquaintances are identical twins, Sharon and Karen. Independent and in their thirties, they share an apartment in Richmond's west end. They share it not only with one another, they discovered, but with one or more nonphysical residents, too. At the twins' invitation, our friend Charles Strickland, Marianne, and I visited their apartment to look for ghosts.

While Marianne and Charles explored the rooms, the twins recounted to me some of the manifestations they had experienced. Karen led off: "When I go to bed at night, something walks the hallways . . . a shuffling noise on the carpet, into my bedroom; then it stops. . . . We occasionally see shadows, darting to and from the hallway for the bedrooms. It's just a little glance; you can't tell that there's [really] something, but you just sense it— you know there's something there."

Sharon agreed. "When we go to bed at night, I hear the [entity] walking down the hall," she said. "It starts right at the hallway and goes straight to Karen's bedroom. I never hear it return. It does not come into my bedroom." As for shadows, Sharon noted, "I see the [shadows] darting in the bedroom, as I wash dishes in the kitchen, all the time. It's as if someone's head is peeking out from the doorway." (Her bedroom doorway is visible from that part of the kitchen.)

The twins share their apartment with two cats, which also seem to sense interlopers. Karen said, "Many times, the cats get up in the middle of the night and growl, for no reason . . . they jerk around like something's in the room."

In confirmation, Sharon added, "We smell a scent . . . sometimes a very, very pungent rose scent, so strong that you can almost taste it down your throat. And then, at times, it can be lilac."

Even a pleasant scent becomes an annoyance when it's too strong. More than an annoyance, though, was another of Sharon's experiences: "One night I did have the sensation of someone being in my bedroom . . . I woke up out of sleep real frightened. It was the most angry feeling I have ever felt. Always before, it was like curiosity, but this one, it was mad at me! And I was home alone."

The twins further agreed on a singular vision of an individual sitting on the floor of their living room, evidently manifesting in great detail, as Karen told us. ". . . [S]hort dark hair, plaid shirt, and dark, navy blue pants," she said. "From the side, it looked like a man, but I knew instinctively it was a woman." Each of the twins saw this figure just once—individually and at different times.

I asked how long these manifestations had been going on and was told eight years—ever since the twins had moved into the apartment, which was new at the time. Since they hadn't been bothered in earlier residences, this seemed to associate the manifestations with the geographic locale, not with attachment to the persons.

At this juncture, Charles and Marianne returned from their exploration of the premises, and I asked what they may have sensed. "An energy—I guess 'restless' is as good a term as any—" Marianne said, "back in [Karen's] bedroom."

"The only qualification I would make to that," Charles added, "would be 'restlessly playful.'"

Marianne demurred. "There are *two* energies," she countered. "One feels restless to me, and one feels playful."

"I can only sense one, in a corner," Charles said, "and that was yellow-pink,[1] and another color I can't pick up. . . . I don't feel any malevolence from it."

"No, I [too] don't feel malevolence," Marianne agreed.

"Mischievous, maybe," Charles concluded.

With this, Marianne prepared to enter trance, while Charles settled back to visualize the usual protective energy field around her. In a few moments, her body began the exploratory stretching-and-feeling motions that signify the entry of a foreign entity essence.

After the accommodation seemed complete, I offered the usual greeting: "Hello."

Only a sigh came forth. "It feels strange to be in a body [again], doesn't it?" I asked, by way of inviting conversation.

More sighs and grunts; then it demanded imperiously, "Who are you?"

I find this question always difficult to handle well. I have this image of a person suddenly waking among a group of total strangers, in puzzlingly foreign surroundings, unaware of the passage of perhaps hundreds of years. My identity means nothing to that person, and the jump in time is incomprehensible, as well; how does one establish rapport?

"I'm a friend," I said simply. Then, seeking his name, I said, "You may call me Bob, if you choose. May I ask who you are?"

---

1. Pink, in Charles's aura color perception, can signify the presence of a childlike energy.

"Simon," he said.

"Simon," I repeated. "Do you have a last name, Simon?"

"What's it to ya?" he retorted, defensively.

"Oh, I'm a very curious person; I will ask a lot of questions, because I'm very ignorant about who you are and where you come from and why you are here."

He wasn't forthcoming with his last name. "Came to get m' dad," he announced.

"Is your dad here? Have you found him?"

"Nay—he was. 'Told him I'd come back for him; I dunno why he didn't stay."

Simon's speech was nasal, with a provincial inflection. Wondering if he were an immigrant, I said, "You sound English, Simon. . . ."

"Nah," he retorted. "I was born right outside of Richmond."

"Oh, really? A native Virginian."

"Yeah," he agreed. "Sarah and I went to Ohio, though. We were going to come back and get Dad."

"I see. So you left Ohio?"

"Just long enough to come back and get Dad."

"So you came back to Richmond," I echoed. "And have you found your dad?"

"Nah!"

If I were to ask further questions in proper context, I needed to know the era we were dealing with. "Answer a question for me. Simon," I asked, "What year is it? I—I've lost track of the date!"

"Year?"

"Yes," I said, "What year is this?"

"Don't read much," he said, as though that explained everything.

I have become accustomed to deceased children and slaves being unaware of dates, but I expected a self-sufficient adult to know. "Well, you certainly know, when New Year's comes around, what new year you've just celebrated," I remonstrated.

"Sarah and I don't do much celebrating," he intoned.

He was evading me. "Simon," I said, "I think you know what year it is."

"What say?" He sounded almost plaintive.

"Well, let's start," I offered, taking it a step at a time. "Is the month May?"

After some deliberation, Simon said, "I think it's June."

"OK. June of what year . . . ?" I left it open-ended for him to fill in. I received only silence.

All right, then, I'd try another tack: "How old are you?"

"Twenty-sev'n," he said. At least he knew that.

"And you are married to . . . ?" Another open-ended question.

"Sarah."

"Do you have children?"

"Yeah, Sarah 'n' me, we've got a boy back at the spread in Ohio."

He was now answering freely. Pressing on, I asked, "Did Sarah come to Richmond with you for your father?"

"Nah."

"You left her behind," I mused, while framing my next question. I still had no time frame. Perhaps if I could determine whether he came by car, train, or stagecoach, it would give me a handle. "So you came alone. How did you come?" I asked. "By stagecoach? Horse? A buggy?"

"Rode," he said tersely.

"Rode what?"

"Horse." Simon certainly didn't waste words.

"You rode a horse—all the way from Ohio!"

"Stopped some," he commented.

"Oh," I chuckled, "I understand that. All right, what's the last thing you remember about riding and arriving in Richmond?"

" 'Twere late—'twere around ... well, I reckon nine, ten o'clock, 'n' I didn't wanta' scare Dad. Went by the old tavern on Scuffle Town Road; I thought I'd go in there and have a drink, and see if any of the old guys were there.... Don't remember much past that."

This last phrase led me to suspect that it was in the tavern that he had met his fate. Robbery, perhaps? "Did you have a lot of money on your person?" I asked.

"Nah. Sarah didn' let me travel with a lot—just enough to get to and from with Dad. We were going to go ahead and bring Dad's old wagon back wi' us."

That ruled out robbery. How about a drunken fight, I wondered. "Did you, uh, drink too much?"

"Didn't have that much money," he said.

"Did you get into a fight?"

He uttered a long sigh. "Well, a guy that had taken a fancy to Sarah some years back was there."

He paused, so I prodded, "What happened?"

"He said some things about her that a man don' take kindly hearin' about his wife—."

I sensed we were coming close to the moment of death. "And what did you do [then]?"

Another sigh, then, "I threw a drink at 'im."

The obvious question: "What did he do then?"

"Don' remember." He sounded like a child afraid to account for his actions. Then, shifting his focus, Simon said, "I don' understand. Who are these people here? And where's Dad?"

Clearly, he was blocking the memory of the moment of his death. I pushed him a bit. "Well," I said, "something happened to you in that bar—uh, that tavern. I imagine that you probably got into a fight.... When you threw the drink at him, what happened? What did he do?"

"Don' know!" he insisted. "Sarah don' like me fightin'."

Robert H. Coddington, author and principal interviewer of ghosts in this book.
(*Courtesy of Robert H. Coddington*)

Marianne Coddington, Higher-self psychic information source and principal vocal channel for troubled ghosts throughout the book.   (*Courtesy of Marianne Coddington*)

Sandie Fairhill, Higher-self psychic information source and vocal channel for ghosts Elizabeth (Ch.4), Alexandra (Ch. 6), Lizzie (Ch. 10), and Miss Agnes (Ch. 13). (*Courtesy of Sandie Fairhill*)

Charles Strickland, Higher-self psychic information source, researcher, and vocal channel for Father Stephen (Ch. 7) and Kenneth (Ch. 9).
(Courtesy of Charles Strickland)

Roger Pile, Ph.D., Mentor and principal interviewer of ghosts Charity (Ch. 4) and Alice (Ch. 6).
(Courtesy of Roger Pile)

Robert and Marianne just
before she entered a trance.
(*Courtesy of Robert Coddington*)

To collaborate in a spirit
rescue, Sandie and Marianne
both go into a trance.
(*Courtesy of Robert Coddington*)

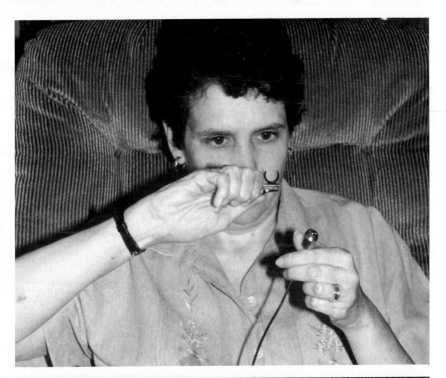

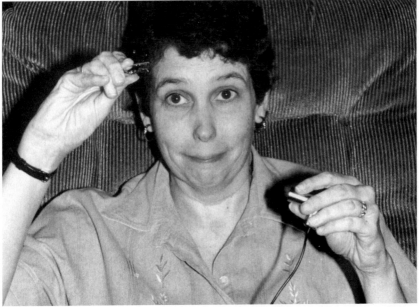

A thirteen-year-old girl who died a century ago, breaks through into wide-eyed temporal awareness, is fascinated by the microphone, and impishly disassembles it. Those who can perceive auras in photographic likenesses may observe the aura surrounding Marianne here differs from her own aura in other photos.
(*Courtesy of Robert Coddington*)

A typical Confederate Civ
War field hospital, similar
the one where Angelica die
while seeking Andrew (Ch. 1, 2
(*Courtesy of the Library of Congre*
and The Museum of the Confederac
Richmond, V

Trains haven't served Main
Street Station in Richmond,
VA for at least twenty years,
but psychic sensitives
gathered there discerned
disturbed energies in the
area. Upon our psychic
invitation from another
location, one manifested
as James Digby (Ch. 8).
The Station, built in 1901,
is about three blocks from
the start of warehouse row,
where Digby ostensibly was
confined.   (*Courtesy of*
Robert Coddington)

A converted colonial tobacco warehouse situated on the James River in Richmond, VA was the site of Libby Prison during the Civil War. Charity sent her daughter Elizabeth here in search of information about the fire (Ch. 4). A previous building on or near this site housed James Digby ninety years earlier (Ch. 8). *(Courtesy of the Library of Congress and The Museum of the Confederacy, Richmond, VA)*

Like Elizabeth MacKenzie (Ch. 4), bereaved survivors wandered through the ruins of burned Richmond. *(Courtesy of the Library of Congress and The Museum of the Confederacy, Richmond, VA)*

The family burial plot i
backyard of private home c
the southern outskirts o
Richmond (Ch. 10). (Courtes
of the present property owne

It is believed this headstone
in the backyard family plot
bearing the name Elizabeth
marks where Lizzie (Ch. 10)
was buried. (Courtesy of
the present property owner)

Georgia Dintelman (Ch. 6, 13), herbalist, once Findhorn resident and student of Native American traditions, served as caretaker of the Oakley Estate in central Virginia. (*Courtesy of the present property owner*)

The main house on the Oakley Estate. (*Courtesy of the present property owner*)

Dr. Wills, Oakley's original owner, conducted his medical practice in this separate building. His daughter Miss Agnes, was his nurse (Ch. 13). (*Courtesy of the present property owner*)

Miss Agnes frequents this stairwell in Oakley House. Marianne clairvoyantly perceived her there, but the camera failed to capture the ghost's image. (*Courtesy of the present property owner*)

Georgia peeks around the door on which Miss Agnes routinely knocked to wake her in the mornings. *(Courtesy of the present property owner)*

Among the headstones in this family burial plot are these identifying Dr. Wills, his wife, his son, and daughter Miss Agnes. *(Courtesy of Robert Coddington)*

Miss Agnes's headstone. (*Courtesy of Robert Coddington*)

"No, but you've done a lot of it, haven't you," I hazarded, "when you were younger?"

Modestly, he responded, "Wouldn' say a lot."

"But you never ran from one, did you?"

"Nah!"

Supposing he may have been ganged up on, I asked, "Even if you were outnumbered, or the other guy had weapons you didn't have?"

A smile crossed Marianne's face. "A fella can duck!"

"You *didn't!*" said a new voice. It came from Charles, who had slipped unnoticed into trance. "Jeremiah shot you, son," it continued, "and you know it."

"Shot me?" Simon sounded genuinely puzzled.

"Right between the eyes."

"Fer throwin' a drink at 'im?" Simon still was incredulous.

I wanted to identify the newcomer. "Who are we . . . ?"

"I am Kenneth," he interrupted. "He knows me."

"Kenneth," I said gratefully, "thanks for coming."

"He were there," Simon announced.

"I watched it," Kenneth confirmed.

To assure myself of the newcomer's intention, I asked, "Kenneth, you have come back to help us, have you?"

"Indeed."

Simon spoke up. "Kenneth, you wouldn't have taken that if they'd said it about Abigail."

"I shot Jeremiah," Kenneth responded, in a flat voice.

I turned again to Simon: "Kenneth certainly is your friend. Do you accept Kenneth as your friend?"

"Yes."

"If Kenneth would tell you that, in fact, you were shot between the eyes that night, and that now you're dead—and have left your own body behind, and that you, Simon, can go on to better places, and rejoin Sarah, and other loved ones, would you believe him?"

" 'Twouldn't be the first time Kenneth had fun with me," he said.

"You wouldn't believe *me,* either, would you?" I posed.

"Nah."

Kenneth spoke again. "I'm not funnin', Simey. They hung me for that."

Simon was disbelieving: "Nay!"

"Oh, yes."

"For a scuffle in a tavern?" Simon was incredulous.

"I *killed* Jeremiah, for killin' you."

"Nah!" Then, suddenly changing his focus, Simon said, "Kenny, where's Dad? He were going to wait here till we got back."

"He's already dead," Kenneth answered. "He died of the fever. You were gone three years."

"Well, he knew Sarah and I were going to get settled there first," Simon defended. " 'Got a nice spread."

"He couldn't help it," Kenneth explained, "he didn't plan to get sick. I was comin' to tell you 'cause I heard you were here— you were seen ridin' in. Only I got there too late."

"I shoulda' writ 'im more," Simon confessed. "I never could write—not good."

I intruded for a parenthetical question of Kenneth: "Can you give me a date?"

His answer, in an aside: "1863."

Back to the chore at hand, I said, "Simon, your father has gone on to his reward; Kenneth has gone to his; and you, Simon, have finished with the lifetime of Simon on this physical plane. What you need to do is to look, to listen, to allow yourself to look for the Light, to look for your loved ones, to listen to their voices and follow them. You can go!"

"You can walk beside me, old friend," Kenneth said.

"Kenneth is here," I continued. "Kenneth will take you by the hand, if you like. . . ."

"Wher' we goin'?" Simon demanded.

Kenneth answered. "To the Light. I've been there."

"Somebody tell Sarah where I am?" Simon entreated.

"She's already there," Kenneth answered.

"And the boy?"

"Yes."

I underlined it. "You'll meet them all . . . and your father."

Still confused, Simon blurted, "I don' understand!"

"You will when you get there," Kenneth explained.

"Will you trust Kenneth, and go with him?" I implored. "You know Kenneth would not harm you. Kenneth, even when he is kidding, is never harmful."

"I'll swear it on the knife," Kenneth asserted.

That got Simon's attention: "On the knife?"

"On the knife."

Simon tested him. "Do you know where the knife is, Kenneth?"

"Yes."

"Where?"

"It's in the oak tree limb that's hollow."

Simon smiled. "You 'membered!"

With Simon's confidence in Kenneth finally solidified, this seemed the moment to push him on. "Go with him and join them," I urged. "You really should go."

Simon asked Kenneth, "What's he talkin' 'bout?"

Charles's body began to shiver. "It's just a little cold for me in here now," Kenneth said, "C'mon with me, where it's warm."

"Cold?" Simon asked.

"Yes." Charles's hand reached to touch Marianne's.

"OK." It was a whisper.

"Go with him!" I exclaimed.

"OK."

They departed. "Godspeed! God be with you. Goodbye," I bade them. "Thank you, Kenneth."

And it was over.

But our ghostly involvement wasn't over! Another learning experience followed immediately. As I waited for Marianne to reassert her own consciousness, suddenly her eyes popped wide open[2] and her countenance changed in the presence of yet another entity—one that was to prove among our most challenging.

The facial expressions and body language of this entity suggested an uninhibited, curious, outgoing, and unafraid personality, almost like a vibrant child. After overcoming my surprise at its unexpected appearance, I tried the usual "Hello?"

There was no response. The expression on Marianne's features was almost impish. "You look like the cat that just swallowed the canary," I said. "Would you tell us your name?"

Still no answer. Instead, she—for we later learned the energy was that of a female—looked around the room curiously, spotted the twins' cat under a cabinet and, with Marianne's body, slid from the chair to reach out to it.[3] The cat regarded her with wide eyes but did not retreat.

I continued to ply her with requests to speak, accused her of

2. Usually a medium channels with eyes closed, but it's not required. In fact, one way to convince a doubting ghost that it has died is to invite it to open the eyes and look at the body it's using, which in most cases is convincingly different from the the entity's former one.

The trance state does not impose limitations on physical movement. We've noted how an emerging entity may explore new physicality through movement of the medium's arms and hands; it's equally possible for the medium to stand and walk about, gesticulate, etc., remaining, all the while, in trance.

3. This was the first time a channeled "outside" personality was allowed actual muscular control of Marianne's body. As it turned out, this bodily control was appropriate to the circumstances.

letting the cat get her tongue, and even appealed to her good manners to respond when spoken to. It took much too long for it to strike me that she might in fact be unable to speak.

This impasse went on for several minutes, when Charles, finally suspecting—or gaining intuitive insight—that she might be deaf as well as mute, took her hand and made an impromptu sign. Instantly, her expression brightened, and she made a sign in return.

Well! So she was a deaf mute. There would be no verbal conversation here. As she and Charles tried to understand one another through his improvised sign language and her responses via Marianne's hands and arms, consternation filled my mind. It never had occurred to me that we'd meet a ghost that couldn't speak, or hear. But of course we could—and clearly had. (True, I had pondered the possibility of meeting a ghost that died as a prespeech infant, or one that spoke no English, but that's never happened to us thus far.) How would we ever get this one to retreat from Marianne's body? Would we have to wait for her to go to sleep? Surely, I thought, Marianne's Higher Consciousness would not allow an "outsider" to remain in control indefinitely. Nevertheless, I sustained a high level of anxiety for the duration of the event.

As I fretted, Charles received more psychic guidance and, after much gesticulating trial and error, finally convinced the entity to vacate Marianne's body and "go" with his own Higher-Self psychic escort. The whole episode ran nearly nine silent minutes, which seemed like hours to me, in my concern for Marianne's return.

It was Charles's impression that he had been communicating with a young American Indian woman. "I simply sensed that [she had] an inability to communicate," he told us later, "and it occurred to me to try sign language. I feel I had some Higher-Self guidance in using it successfully."

Since the only record of the episode was nine minutes of tape with no voice but mine, we later asked Marianne to engage her psychic source to clarify what had happened. Here's what we learned from her SC:

The silent visitor was, as Charles was perceiving from [his Higher Self] during the episode, a fairly young Native American Mattaponi [nation or tribe], mid-1400s. She was born both deaf and mute. She was the daughter of one of the tribe's healers, [and] always looked on as certainly "different" by the rest of the tribe. Because of her parentage, they didn't know whether to see her silence as some kind of a spiritual omen or some kind of curse.

Because of her silence and her strangeness to the tribe, her name would literally interpret to "Child of the Moon." She was impregnated by a cousin—it was an arranged union. She was thirteen. She had a very slight build and was not anatomically prepared to carry twins. She survived the birth of the twins long enough to start nursing them; what they didn't realize at the time, after the delivery, was that she had started to have a massive internal hemorrhage from the [birth], and she very quietly lost consciousness and died while nursing her twin daughters.

Her energy never really left the area, which was right there around [the twins' apartment complex]. It got very much reactivated, however, by [the arrival of twins Karen and Sharon]. The Spirit stayed up until that time in the woods behind the apartments. She had always been at one with nature—she's not an unhappy Spirit; just one that chose not to leave, enjoying being around the trees, the flowers, watching the gradual progress of time. But the sight of the twins, when they moved in there, reawakened something else in her, so she just simply attached herself to them at that point and has been there in the apartment pretty much since they moved in.

It's certainly not a malevolent energy, not an unhappy energy. She did "go over" for a time, when Charles led her over, but she goes back and forth at will. She does not have to reincarnate at this time, and is still enjoying being around the earth energies. So [Karen and Sharon] may see her from time to time; if so, it's because she's there voluntarily.

Child of the Moon is not a "trapped" soul, in the sense that we use it, but is one of those who has the liberty to tarry on this plane for time, if she so chooses. Clearly, she enjoys sharing the apartment with Sharon and Karen.

In reflecting on our experiences with these two entities, Marianne's memories were skeletal. "The twins' apartment certainly was [psychically] comfortable enough," she said. "I was aware of an energy floating through the place, as well as a sense of confusion—which must have been Simon's. I was also aware of a very childlike energy that seemed to stay around the cats there, so I knew there were [at least] two energies there; I didn't know whether both were going to be coming through.

"I really don't remember much, and I don't remember their taking any toll on the body. I don't have the feeling, upon coming out of trance, of having been stressed."

Since it had appeared that Child of the Moon entered Marianne the instant Simon left, I asked if she had any conscious recollection of the change of energies. "No," she answered. "I was only aware of the overall time loss." It is interesting to note that, although we understand Child of the Moon to be an aware entity, here by choice rather than unaware, Marianne had no partial consciousness during trance, such as she has experienced with other aware entities.

* * *

It's our understanding that Simon did, in fact, move on to the next realm, while Child of the Moon exercises her option to remain on the earth plane, for the present. Neither of these entities accounts for the woman in blue pants and plaid shirt that Karen and Sharon saw at different times. Marianne suspects this one may be an example of the "apparitional haunting," defined in the first chapter: the remaining psychic record of a past event that manifests as a repetitive "movie" tableau; a psychic energy pattern without consciousness or volition.

There's not much explicit detail in these episodes usable for seeking corroboration. Regarding Simon's story, there was an early-settled area, west of the city proper of that time and now well within it, which was in fact called Scuffle Town, and there was a Scuffle Town Road.[4]

Then there's the question of Simon's traveling from Ohio, the north, to Confederate Richmond in 1863—a time when battle fronts were heavily defended and moving daily. Simon made no mention of hostilities, challenges, delays, or traveling covertly. Was it possible, at the height of the war, for a civilian resident of one territory to cross freely into "enemy" territory, intending to return on family business? Unfortunately, Kenneth's revelation of the date came too late in our dialog to raise this crucial question with Simon.

Regarding his channeling of Kenneth, Charles, as usual, was

4. Julia Cuthbert Pollard, *Richmond's Story* (Richmond, Virginia: Richmond Public Schools, 1954). Scuffle Town was in the area of Richmond's Grove Avenue and Mulberry Street today, and Scuffle Town Road, eastbound to the city proper of that time, is Park Avenue today. Since one historian refers to troops marching along Scuffle Town Road to reach Westhampton, a few miles west of Scuffle Town, it appears the road also extended to the west under that name and probably was one route into Richmond from that direction. Surely, it would have had taverns along the way. The twins' apartment is on the order of eight miles nominally west of the old Scuffle Town area.

ignorant of the dialog's content but did recall an emotional involvement with Simon during his presence. "It wasn't the all-embracing sense of love of all humanity that I felt with Father Stephen." Charles said, "It was more the supportive, focused, fraternal love one feels for a close friend."

As for Child of the Moon, nothing came of our encounter, itself for possible verification. We have only the information Marianne received psychically, and even that is minimal. It's true that Mattaponi (sometimes Mattapony) Native Americans, with their language rooted in Algonquian, once flourished in Virginia. Their legacy is visible today: for instance, in the names of several Virginia rivers. Since Native Americans in general date as much as two thousand years in the past, it's reasonable to accept that Child of the Moon lived in the fifteenth century.

It's fascinating to note that scholars have estimated there were at least two hundred different languages and dialects among the aborigines of North America. Intertribal communication may not have been as difficult as one would suppose; Collier's Encyclopedia notes that "In North America an unusual language form existed [in certain areas]; by means of numerous hand signs, many tribes with mutually unintelligible languages could easily converse with one another."[5] Perhaps Child of the Moon's handicap presented little problem to her tribal peers, after all.

One interesting aside: Many researchers of the paranormal report strange and inexplicable failures of technical equipment—notably cameras, and audio and video recorders—as though certain psychic energies somehow interfere with them. Generally, I have not encountered this failure phenomenon, even though I have dealt extensively with both professional and commercial audio tape recorders, since their general availability in the late

5. *Collier's Encyclopedia* (New York: Crowell-Collier Educational Corporation, 1968). Volume 12, p. 648.

1940s (and video recorders since the 1970s). However, a technical dysfunction did occur during this particular evening of channeling which, while it may have been pure chance, occurred with a peculiar coincidence of timing.

I was using two clip-on microphones—one on Marianne and the other on Charles. Upon playback of the tape, all had recorded well—until the moment when Simon left Marianne and Child of the Moon abruptly slipped in. At the very instant of this sudden change of energies, one of the microphones (which one is indeterminate) abruptly generated a sharp burst of static on the tape. The noise continued in sporadic outbreaks of progressively diminishing intensity for about the next minute, after which everything settled down and functioned entirely normally for the balance of the evening's action—even though the mostly silent sign language, from that point on, rendered it useless, anyway. Coincidence? Or some electromagnetic disturbance intruding from an overlap of two greatly dissimilar energies and Marianne's wrenching adjustment to the change? Was a technological sound problem somehow symbolic of Child of the Moon's inability to hear or speak?

We'll never know.

10
GHOSTLY GOSSIPS

Perhaps—excepting closemouthed Melinda and mute Child of the Moon—the ghosts of the preceding chapters were what we informally call "trapped," or "earthbound" souls, ignorant of their decease and emotionally stuck in their moment of impending death. As discussed in Chapter 1, though, we've understood that not all ghosts remain here through blind ignorance; it's said some know full well they are discarnate but nevertheless voluntarily inhabit this plane, for one reason or another. We finally met a pair clearly fitting this description—an amusing pair, it turned out—at the home of Pat and Mike.

Pat was, at the time, a fellow nursing student with Marianne. When she learned of our interest in ghosts, she remarked that strange things happened at their home. Perhaps we'd be interested in checking it out?

Of course. In fact, our whole Metaphysical Research Group would be interested. So one August evening, fifteen of us filled Pat and Mike's comfortable home on the southern outskirts of Richmond.

For those in the group who hadn't heard Pat's earlier tales, she reviewed many strange things she and her family had experienced during the several years they had lived in the house. "It first started when we moved into the house, which was in July of 1975," she related. "At that time, we thought we had an electrical problem, because lights would start coming on and going off [spontaneously]. Michael checked out the electrical system, and there wasn't anything wrong.

"Then, come Christmas, Michelle [a daughter] started telling me she had a guardian angel that talked with her at night. I just thought it was a typical eight year old's imagination.

"We would leave—go out—and come back, and the [electric] candle in her bedroom would be on. We checked numerous times to make sure it was unplugged [before leaving], and come back to find it plugged in and on.

"Then we began feeling a presence in the living room area. It was like someone would come by and put a hand on your shoulder—something like that. And this oval-shaped mirror behind me was in the dining room, and every now and then we'd catch shadows going back and forth [in it]."

Unnerving as all this must have been to Pat and Mike, it was exceeded by their vacation experience the following summer: "We were camping, while the dog [and rabbits, at home] were supposed to have been taken care of by a friend. . . . Well, I got a phone message at the camp ground to call home—our home phone number. We couldn't figure it out; we had checked earlier and found out the friend was out of town and had never got here. But when Michael got here, the dog had been fed, the rabbits had food and water, and none of the neighbors had taken care of them! In fact, one of the neighbors had tried to come into the back yard, and the dog got very vicious with her and wouldn't let her in the yard. [Even though there had been a terrible storm while we were gone] the dog wasn't muddy, the food was dry, and the water was cool. When we got the telephone bill, there was a call from my house to [the camp ground]—we never found out who made it, though."

Mysterious happenings, indeed! Someone in our group wondered aloud if Pat found them at all threatening.

She started to admit: "I got a little . . . uh—I never was frightened, though," she finally declared. "It never was like there was anything in the house that was doing harm." She then revealed that she had gone to a psychic about it and was told that whoever was in the house was a "good spirit," and there was nothing to worry about.

"Well, there were so many little things happening that I just didn't pay any attention to it after that," Pat told us. "And then something tried to materialize in the dining room one night, and the dog came over to me, cowering down and whimpering. I just got up and left—I didn't stick around to see what it was. At that point in the game, I just said, 'I believe you're here, that's nice. I like you. Goodbye!' and went straight upstairs to the bedroom."

On another occasion, during a heated discussion between Pat and Mike, when they were home alone, Pat suddenly heard the piano in the family room below. "It was just three notes: dah, dah, dum," she said. "I went downstairs and the piano [keyboard] cover was still down."

Other inexplicable events in the house included: the sound of breaking glass, for which no cause could be found, toilets flushing spontaneously in the middle of the night, peripheral glimpses by several in the family of fleeting shadows. While visiting the family, Pat's father plainly saw all the bathroom towels spirited off their racks and dumped into the tub, which raised in him the need for a drink; when he went to the refrigerator, he found its door already open for him—so he took *two* drinks.

All this ghostly activity puzzled Pat because they had bought the house new; no one else had lived in it. However, we learned there were five graves in a plot enclosed by an iron fence in the back yard, not an uncommon rural sight in this area, but rare in suburbs. In a bygone era, families often had burial plots on their plantation, estate, or farm. The wrought-iron fences and gates served to keep out livestock. The graves here implied that there had been an earlier house on the grounds, and indeed, Pat told us, there once was a farm where their home stands today.

We stepped out and explored the diminutive cemetery. Pat had researched the early family and the members buried there. The most recent burial was in 1902, while at least two stones dated back to the Civil War era. Marianne stepped inside the fence and read those headstones that were still legible. We then returned to the house.

Some of the happenings Pat related suggested some degree of interactive awareness, so we suspected that whatever entity, or entities, residing there was there by choice, not blind fixation. We already understood there is such a thing as an aware ghost, although we hadn't interacted with any at that stage of our experience. We were eager to do so. Here, as we prepared to contact them, we didn't expect emotionally heavy confrontations, such as we had with Angelica and Effie. Neither did we expect a comedy team.

Marianne and friend, Sandie Fairhill, sat on the couch, and, while the rest of us speculated impatiently, they both slipped into trance states. Both? Were we in for a *pair* of ghosts? Whispering among ourselves, we wondered how to address the entity, or entities, we were expecting.

Before we could settle anything, someone spoke through Marianne: "Well?"

"Hello," I said, as warmly as I could. This met with silence, so I amplified: "Good evening. You're among friends here tonight."

"I know that."

"I'm sure you do," I agreed. Acting on our initial assumption,

I said, "If I understand it correctly, you are here of your own choice. Is that right?"

"Both Elizabeth and I are."

So we were right: ghosts were here in pairs tonight. "May I ask why? Would you tell us a little story of what the two of you are doing here—what draws you here?"

"I like it here." As if this were reason enough.

"And what is *your* name, by the way?" I asked.

"Hester Rose Irene Walker Marshall," was her cadenced reply.

I rolled the names around on my tongue: "Hester Rose Irene Walker Marshall!"

"I've always been called Rosie."

"And is this Elizabeth, next to you, who's sitting there smiling?"

"Yes."

I thought she may as well join the party. "Do you think she would speak to us?" I asked Rosie.

Rosie said the obvious: "Ask her."

So I did. "Good evening, Elizabeth."

"Good evening." Her voice was a near-whisper.

"It's very nice of you to visit us this evening, Elizabeth," I welcomed her. "Would you tell us your name—as completely as Rosie did?"

"Just call me Lizzie," she retorted.

"All right—it's Lizzie and Rosie. Do you have any connection with the small cemetery out back? Either of you?"

Lizzie said, "About as much connection as anyone could have."

"Lizzie's there; I'm not," Rosie explained. "They took me back to my husband's home, to be buried next to him."

Seeking clues to her mortal existence, I asked, "And where was that?"

"Fluvanna County [Virginia]."

"And what was your age then, Rosie? When you died."

"I was eighteen."

I hadn't expected her death so young. "You were eighteen? Do you know the year?"

"Yes," was all Rosie said. Discarnates can sometimes be infuriatingly literal in their interpretation of a question.

"Well?"

"I died in 1769," she responded.

"Thank you." I turned to the other medium. "Lizzie? Some of your remains lie in the cemetery out back, do they?"

Lizzie passed it off lightly: "Only what I no longer needed."

"Of course," I agreed. "At what age did you [Lizzie] meet your mortal end?"

She suddenly turned coy. "Oh . . . I don't wanta' tell you."

"Oh, I'm sorry," I said, in exaggerated tones of apology, "Excuse me for prying into a lady's age. Can you tell me the year?"

Clearly Lizzie took pride in being evasive: "I forget . . . I don't want to think about those things." Changing the subject quickly, she gushed, "It's so-o nice—this was such a *good* idea!"

"*I* think so," Rosie seconded.

I began to feel manipulated. "Whose idea was this?"

"Oh, we all got together . . .," Lizzie explained.

"Uh-huh. . . . I thought so," I noted.

Lizzie began to hit her stride. "Do you have *any* idea how *lo-ong* it's been since we could just sit and talk with people?"

"Well," I countered, "they keep telling us that beyond the physical, time really has no meaning."

"Nonsense!" Rosie retorted.

Lizzie rambled on: "See, we really enjoy sitting and talking—*especially* talking about other people. And it's kind of difficult to get your point across sometimes, when people can't really hear you . . . or see you."

"We *try* to help," Rosie interjected.

"Yeah, we sure do," Lizzie echoed.

Listening to these two characters snapping up cues from each other, as though they were scripted, reminded me of the Brewster sisters in a noted stage play. "Why do I feel like I'm listening to *Arsenic and Old Lace?*" I disgressed, with a chuckle. Someone among the group whispered, "I was just thinking the same thing!"

Then, getting back on course, I asked, "So you do what we normally consider poltergeist sorts of things to get your point across—is this what I'm understanding?"

"No," Rosie said.

"No? Then you tell me."

"Well, I think we both try to *help*," Rosie answered. "I remember one night—oh, lands . . . maybe two, three years ago—Pat was crying and crying over something somebody had said to her, and I went over and put both my hands on her shoulders, and I tried so hard to let her know it was OK. I just couldn't . . . just couldn't make her understand."

"It's sometimes difficult to communicate," Lizzie affirmed, "but you know, there are so many times when we really try to help, and it doesn't go *quite* the way we expected. You see, we sometimes have a little problem with coordination, since we don't have physical bodies anymore. . . . And sometimes when we intend to help—maybe by moving something—it kinda' slips and just takes off. You know what I mean?"

"Not by experience that I can recall," I replied, "but I'll accept your explanation."

"Well," Lizzie concluded, "it doesn't always go where it's supposed to go. Or the way it's supposed to go."

Understanding these discarnates to be on this plane voluntarily, I wanted to know why. "Ordinarily, most people—as we understand it—when they come to the end of their mortal experience here, manage to move on to other levels. . . ." I began.

"Oh, we've been there," Rosie interrupted.

"You've been there? Well, yes, we understand you're here by choice. I guess I'm looking for a little more information about what has drawn you to this particular spot—this particular house, which is not a traditional haunted house at all."

"Well, I tried to help little Charlie's wife," Rosie explained, obliquely, "and she didn't want me there. I think she resented me. But I'd let her know in the night when the baby was wet, when the baby needed feeding, and she really resented me. This was my home, so I came back here."

I didn't know who little Charlie was, or his wife, or how they related to my question. "Who is little Charlie's wife?" I asked.

"Had I survived, she would have been my daughter-in-law. Eleanor Shelton. Her family was from Charleston, and they always thought they knew better. Charlie should have married good Virginia stock."

Lizzie couldn't resist. "They *always* look down on other people. With their hoity-toity ideas! They're really pretty disgusting people."

"That's true," Rosie confirmed. "I don't know why Charlie married a Shelton."

To my mild surprise, there came a lull in their conversation. I took advantage of it to suggest questions from our group. "I have the feeling," I ventured, "that either of you ladies would be delighted to converse and carry on with anyone here."

Lizzie almost whispered, "Especially if it's gossipy!"

After the laughter passed, someone asked, "Who plays the piano?"

"We both were certainly trained to play, as young ladies," Rosie answered. "Lizzie does play better, though."

"That's something else that doesn't always come out quite the way I want it," Lizzie added. "Sometimes I just am ten thumbs, ya' know."

Another question from the group: "Where are you from, Lizzie?"

"Oh, I'm good Richmond stock. I wouldn't live anywhere else."

Phil Fairhill, the historian in our group, was interested in details. "Do you know what kind of piano it was?" he asked. "Was it an upright?"

"Which piano?" Lizzie inquired.

"The one that you trained on."

Rosie said, "*I* trained on a harpsichord."

"My piano," Lizzie boasted, "was brought from Europe by my father."

Phil pressed on, trying to establish when Lizzie lived: "I can't gossip if I don't know the year."

"You'll find out the year. . . . You know what questions to ask," Lizzie said, archly.

"Lizzie was older when she died, and she's very sensitive about her age," Rosie chided.

"She only *thinks* I was older. I *never* got old," Lizzie declared.

"Did you ever marry?"

Lizzie sighed deeply. "No."

"I'll bet you had a lot of suitors," the historian ventured.

"Till Daddy chased them all away."

"I presume, then, they weren't from Virginia?"

"No," Lizzie continued, "you see, at that time, good Virginia boys were difficult to find. They were all running off and getting themselves killed in the war."

"When was the last one driven into Lee's army by your father?" the historian asked.

Another sigh from Lizzie. "On the eve of our [intended] wedding," she said, sadly.

There followed several minutes of pointed questions by the historian about Lizzie's travels and activities during her lifetime. He was seeking to relate them to known historical persons of the

Civil War and to certain associated relics in local museums. While he succeeded to his own satisfaction, I shall spare you the details of that digression.

Then someone asked Rosie a question: "Is there a possibility of a sketch, drawing, or painting of you existing somewhere?"

"Not that I know of," she said.

"Ro-o-sie," Lizzie admonished. "You know—"

"I never felt *that* was a good likeness, Lizzie," Rosie snapped.

"But it does exist," Lizzie insisted. "If you can tell on *me*, I can tell on *you!*"

"You're a goose, Lizzie!"

This argument rambled on aimlessly for a few moments. Then someone asked for any messages Rosie or Lizzie might have for Pat and Mike, their mortal hosts.

"Well, we've thoroughly enjoyed being here," Lizzie responded. "Part of the reason we enjoy it so much is, not only because we're familiar with the area and like it here, but the people here have been delightful. They've accepted us and what we do. . . ."

Rosie interrupted. "Pat's father didn't. You shouldn't have frightened him that night, Lizzie."

"He was being a cantankerous old fool!" Lizzie snorted. "He wouldn't answer me. You *know* how I hate being ignored."

The questioning returned to Rosie. Someone asked about her mortal life, what she did, and why she's here now.

"I feel like I'm accomplishing some with the existence I'm in now," she began. "It's not always easy without the ability of direct communication, but I—I try."

"Besides," Lizzie interjected, mischievously, "she couldn't eavesdrop as well, if she were physical."

"There is, of course, something to that," Rosie conceded.

Next question: "What kind of life did you live, Rosie?"

"Oh, it was pleasant enough. Life in the colonies was not always easy, but my family situation was comfortable. I married Charlie Marshall when I was seventeen.

"Charlie and I didn't have very long together," she continued, " 'cause I died in giving birth to little Charlie. But I've always particularly enjoyed being around children, and I love animals, and I have sought out families where I can be of use with children and animals—and, OK, Lizzie, sometimes I get involved."

Lizzie had been quiet as long as she could stand. "You didn't tell about all those cute soldiers before Charlie. . . ."

"Yes," Rosie admitted, "there were wars going on with the Indians out west, and we certainly saw some [soldiers] come through this area."

One of the men asked, "Did you know George Washington?"

"No, I never met Mr. Washington personally."

It was Pat's turn to question her: "Is that one of the reasons you chose to be in our household so often—because of all the children and animals?"

"Yes," Rosie said, "and my parents' farm had been here, so this felt like home. And when you and Mike and the children—and the dogs—and the rabbits—were all here, etcetera, etcetera, it felt good, and it felt comfortable, and I like being around the children."

"Did you feed the dogs, Rosie, when [the vacation caretaker] was gone?"

"Certainly. Someone had to! . . . The dogs know I'm here."

We had some meandering discussion about discarnates moving physical objects and sometimes being visible. This prompted Rosie to comment: "It is, incidentally, generally Lizzie that's seen in front of mirrors."

"Yes," Lizzie conceded, "aren't they a *marvelous* thing?"

"Is Lizzie vain?" someone asked, as though we hadn't already inferred as much.

It must have been with tongue-in-cheek that she replied, "Of course not!"

At least Rosie didn't buy it. "Go ahead, you goose—tell the truth."

"I enjoy mirrors. That does *not* mean I'm vain."

It's commonly believed by some that a ghost which may be directly visible to the human eye isn't visible in a mirror. This prompted the next question: "Lizzie, can you see yourself in a mirror?"

"I see what I *wish* to see in a mirror."

Which spurred Rosie to exclaim, "She did, even when she was alive!"

Someone else, perceiving some visiting discarnates lurking about, asked, "How many of you live here with Pat and Mike?"

"We don't really *live* here," Lizzie explained. "We just, uh, 'pop in' from time to time."

"Where do you spend the rest of your time?" someone wanted to know.

"Here . . . and there . . . visiting . . . ," she evaded.

"Do [you two] intend to stay?" someone else asked.

"Certainly," Rosie said.

And, so far as I know, they did and have. We certainly left Pat and Mike's home with the understanding that Lizzie and Rosie would continue to "pop in" from time to time, as whim might dictate.

After our emotionally heavy interactions with Angelica, Effie, Molly, and others, the droll banter and posturing of these two "aware" characters made this a delightful change among our ghost experiences. It's impossible to convey in print the inflections and vocal nuances of the dry "zingers" Rosie and Lizzie fired at each other; suffice it to say that the session frequently was punctuated by our laughter. It was also long; many of its least entertaining or illustrative digressions are omitted here.

This episode was different in another way. Marianne said afterward, "I was [mostly] aware of what was going on, while it was going on. I think this is because Rosie and Lizzie were fully aware entities, not 'trapped' souls in distress. They certainly were there by choice."

This increased awareness of Marianne's gave her some direct perception of the personality she was channeling. "I remember Rosie being a very 'cozy' energy," she related. "Rosie coming in to speak through my body was kind of like somebody settling into a nice, comfortable chair—maybe in an unfamiliar home, but a comfortable chair, to sit down and have a nice, comfortable chat. [I found it] a very comfortable experience. Just two gossipy ladies, very happy to have somebody to listen to them. I had no sense at all of their being 'released,' but I don't think they had any desire [or need] to be."

Phil, with his remarkable knowledge of Civil War-era details, had asked Lizzie a number of pointed questions. From her answers, he found Lizzie's tale to closely fit certain facts and events in local Confederate history, supportive of her validity. Though we had explicit names and dates, we made no follow-up effort to find corroborating evidence of Rosie's and Lizzie's physical existences.

This episode clearly demonstrates the distinction between an "earthbound" soul that is ignorant of its physical death and the passage of time in our reality, and one who is aware, who perhaps has gone on to other planes and has chosen (and is free) to come back to this one, for one reason or another. Even though they had lived and died in widely separated times, Rosie and Lizzie met each other in their nonphysical states, interacted, and became friends. They were both aware of Pat and Mike and their family, pets, and surroundings and tried to interact with them in the context of the present. Compare this with Angelica, Effie, Alice, and several others in this book, and the term "free spirit" takes on a new meaning.

11

GROUNDED BY GRIEF

We saw in the previous chapter that some earth-residing ghosts are conscious of their mortal demise. A few, like Rosie and Lizzie, may remain (or return) here by choice. However, in the episode presented here, we learned from Evan[1] that others, though aware of their mortal death, can be psychically chained to the earth plane by surviving mortals.

It was Evan's mother, Rose,[1] who approached us for help. Evan, in his late teens, and some friends had gone swimming in a small lake one evening several months before. Although he could swim and was in good health, he somehow had drowned, and she, distraught in her struggle to accept the stark reality of his death, was suspicious of the circumstances behind the tragedy. It was her hope that we might contact his surviving essence and gain from him reassurance concerning certain details of his final moments. We agreed to help, if we could.

It was on a chilly February evening that Marianne and I met

---

1. "Evan" and "Rose" are pseudonyms. Some details have been changed to preserve the principals' anonymity.

with Rose and Lou Ebersole at Lou's apartment. Also present was Lou's son, Don. We settled in for a briefing.

Rose rambled at length, recalling how difficult it remained, these many months since his death, for her to accept it. She felt certain Evan had manifested to her in dreams and reveries, telling her he was dead and had to go on, yet she remained unable to reconcile herself to the fact.

In the course of our discussion, it came to light that Rose and a friend had been seeking an explanation for Evan's tragedy through a Ouija board,[2] a practice greatly adding to her extreme difficulty in coping with Evan's death. The board had spelled out messages professing to be from Evan himself, alleging that he was the victim of murder. "He" said he was hit on the head with a rock while in the water and was knocked unconscious. Indeed, there were contusions on Evan's body, Rose told us, but she conceded these could reasonably be attributed to other known events preceding the drowning. Nevertheless, because the Ouija board's "he" had urged Rose to call in a detective to investigate his death, she couldn't shake her suspicion of foul play.

She brought some of Evan's personal belongings to us. One was a tape with his voice, which she hoped might give us an insight into his personality and help us establish a rapport with his Spirit. Since Marianne can perceive one's aura from the sound of his or her voice, this did in fact provide her with an initial impression.

Rose carried on at length about Evan's likes and dislikes, accomplishments and failures, and his friends and acquaintances.

2. The Ouija, or talking board, is one on which all the letters of the alphabet and the numbers, from 0 to 9, are arrayed, as are the words "yes," "no," "hello," and "good bye." A pointer called the planchette is lightly held by one or two persons and is allowed to move about the board to spell out messages. "Ouija" is a registered trademark of Parker Brothers Company, which sells the product as a parlor game.

She handed personal items of Evan's to Lou and Don—both psychometrists[3]—for any psychic impressions they might obtain from them. She even had photos of his grave marker and of the funeral proceedings. Clearly, Rose's grief had pushed her into a consuming obsession.

Upon first handling Evan's ring, Don announced, "Your son wasn't murdered." As he fingered other items and studied photos, he reaffirmed this, with high certainty, several times. Lou and Marianne concurred with him.

Having only sketchy details of Evan's accident, Rose pressed for specific information, seeking more assurance that no foul play was involved. After ordering his scattered impressions, Don gave her a detailed scenario as he perceived it:

> Somebody was playing—play-acting—goofing around in the middle of the lake. The way it appears to me is that your son mistakenly thought that they were in trouble, and he went out to help. When he was getting close, the person acting just turned around and innocently swam away from him toward shore. Your son just wasn't strong enough to make it back, and when the others realized it, they couldn't get back to him in time.

While he was relating this, I saw that Marianne's eyes had closed, as if to go into trance. Thinking it premature, I tried to stop her: "Marianne!"

I was too late. The person who spoke was not Marianne. "Mama, I can't go on till you let go. Let go!" The voice broke with sorrow.

---

3. As noted in Chapter 1, a psychometrist may receive psychic impressions of a person or their circumstances by holding and concentrating on some item of that person's.

"Evan?" My question was rhetorical; I knew it was he.

Ignoring me, he blurted, "It was an accident. Let go! Oh, please let go."

I turned to assure Rose. "This is Evan."

Persons new to channeling are often awed by the emerging personality. Whispering, she hesitantly asked if she could speak directly to him.

"Surely."

Evan resumed, before she could respond. "Mama, I know you love me, but you have to let me go."

Rose's impassioned sob spoke eloquently of her difficulty in letting him go.

"I know, Mama. . . . I know it's hard. But please—I've got to go!"

Still clinging to Evan's presence, Rose blurted questions through her tears. Did he hurt in death? Did he really visit her in her dreams?

"No, Mama, I didn't hurt. I did come to you. . . . Mama, I've *gotta* go." Then, aware of her lingering suspicion of foul play, Evan added, "Mama, it was just an accident."

Would his simple declaration satisfy her? I suspected Rose still harbored some doubt. "Evan," I interjected, "may we reinforce one thing beyond any question? You were *not* murdered, were you?"

Without hesitation, he declared, "No, sir."

"Your death was entirely accidental?" I pressed.

"Yes, sir."

"And so there is no one to blame. . . ."

"No, sir." He paused, then, imploringly, "Oh, Mama, the light's there and I want to go to it. Let go of me." His voice rose in an anguished outburst, unintelligible on the tape.

Rose sat speechless, tears still coursing down her cheeks. "Go with our love," I offered, in benediction. "God bless you." And with a great sigh, he was gone.

The intensely emotional experience of speaking with her recently dead son, and having so reluctantly to let go of him, left Rose understandably in copious tears. Lou and Don moved to comfort her, while I tended to Marianne as she emerged from trance. She had no memory of the conversation, of course, but she was physically shaken by being host to one so distraught and sorrowful. It would take a few moments for her to regain normal composure.

Digesting and reflecting on the episode, Rose finally seemed convinced that Evan had indeed come to her in dreams to plead for release. "Yes," I elaborated. "He needed to go. Your strong desire to hold on to him, to reverse his death, and your suspicions about the circumstances were all holding him back. You did a great thing today—a great act of love—by listening to him, and giving him 'permission' to go."

Recognizing that Rose still desperately needed to put the past behind her, Lou called upon her counseling experience to proffer advice. "Rose, let me make a suggestion," she said. "Take all these things—all these mementoes—and put them in a box. Wrap them up; wrap them in red paper, and put them away."

"It's *so* hard!" Rose lamented.

"You've let him go," Lou continued, "Now take all these things and wrap them up and put them away."

Marianne, now fully functional, added, "The other thing you need to do is to get in touch with Compassionate Friends, because it's time for you to start to heal. Evan is happy where he is. He is at peace, but *you* need to heal now."

This went on for some time, Rose reliving her hurt and confusion, over and over, while we strove to ease her into a focus on the present and future. I concluded it was easier in this instance to bring healing to the dead than to the living.

We gave her a further suggestion—one we make to all who dabble as amateurs with Ouija boards: Burn them! While the Ouija board may be nothing more than a harmless game for some, it's our experience that for others, it can be an indiscriminate invitation to discarnate beings—and not all discarnates are benign. It has brought troubling energies to unsuspecting experimenters, including some of our acquaintance.

An extreme instance of the board's role as an invitation to negative energies underlies the book and movie, *The Exorcist*. According to a Roman Catholic priest familiar with the life of the real boy whose affliction was the inspiration for the fictionalized story, the troubles started when the boy began consulting a Ouija board.[4]

Given that Rose had initially accepted her board's pronouncements as valid, her angry state of extreme tumult is understandable, not to mention her confusion when she heard an entirely different story from Evan, as manifested by Marianne. It's no wonder that she was torn with doubt, suspicion, confusion, and grief in her quest for reassurance. Which postmortem "Evan" should she believe?

We explored this. Those psychically sensitive—Marianne, Lou, and Don—agreed that the Evan we had heard that evening was genuine. Upon reflection, Rose herself finally confirmed it, having convincingly felt, during the session, that she was truly in touch with her son's personality through Marianne.

This leads inescapably to the conclusion that the entity manifesting through her Ouija board was, in fact, an imposter, a being

4. As related by the Reverend John Nicola, M.A., Technical Consultant for the film *The Exorcist*, in an address at Northern Virginia Community College, Sterling, Virginia, March 28, 1981.

who claimed, for whatever obscure reason, to be Evan and delighted in deeply troubling Rose. Clearly, discarnate imposters are opportunists to be avoided.

This episode marked another step in our education about ghosts. As Marianne recounted, "[The case of] Evan was a different thing, altogether. To begin with, I did not anticipate channeling Evan. I only did so after all our efforts to coerce his mother to let go of him failed. While we were urging her to no avail, it was almost as if I sensed this Spirit 'knocking at the door' to be heard. Finally, since nothing else had worked, in desperation [my Higher Self] and I allowed it to come through, although I think it was unusual—and probably not very smart—to let somebody as newly transcended as Evan was to come through [to the bereaved]." By this last observation, she explained, based on her professional expertise as hospice nurse to terminally ill patients and their families, how the emotionally necessary processing of one's bereavement may be delayed and prolonged by establishing an unhealthy, clinging, interactive relationship with the deceased.

"The emotion I was aware of with Evan," she continued, "— the difference here is that I was semi-aware during the time Evan was there; I was not as 'out of it' as I usually am during a rescue— I do remember a sense of frustration on Evan's part, because he sensed his mother wasn't really listening to him."

This experience with Evan gave us firsthand confirmation that a soul, even though aware of its physical death, can be held to this plane by the refusal of surviving loved ones to let it go. Apparently the emotional energies coming from an intense desire to hold onto the deceased one can, in fact, inhibit an appropriate departure of the deceased for the next phase of existence. It's as though by wishing strongly enough for a reality, a nonphysical shadow of that reality is created, to the detriment of a nonphysical soul caught in it. Marianne often has observed that a terminally ill patient, who is physically and emotionally ready to pass on, seems to be held in the physical too long by well-meaning family members who passionately and repeatedly implore him or her not to die.

The lesson here, of course, is to mourn appropriately the loss of a loved one, but not to strive to hold them to you inappropriately—not when they need to move on to the next realm. The most loving thing you can do for one ready to pass on is to bid them to "go for the Light," with your blessings. Cherish and cling to the memories, but let the soul go.

12

AFRAID OF HELL

The rambling letter ended with a plea. "I was told you might be able to help me." It was signed Tony Hendrix.[1] Thus began one of our most challenging episodes.

The letter was to Marianne and me from an obviously troubled young man of twenty. It was comprised of five densely filled, typewritten pages detailing the circumstances of his plight. He reported that he had initially written to Roger Pile, who had by then returned to Connecticut. Roger had referred him to us, since the young man lived in our area.

With its wealth of autobiographical and experiential detail, this letter afforded us considerably more background than we usually had before engaging in conversation with a ghost. We learned that Tony had been psychically sensitive since adolescence, having experienced many poltergeist-like happenings that he came in time to attribute to "spirits."

It was Tony's interest and ingenuous dabbling in metaphysics

---

1. A pseudonym. Principals' names and identifying details have been changed to preserve anonymity.

that led to the predicament prompting his letter. As he related, he had visited relatives overseas a year before, where he and a cousin, engaged in a discussion about parapsychology, decided to attempt contact with the cousin's deceased grandfather. With several relatives present, they sat expectantly around a homemade Ouija board, inviting something to happen. It did.

We view the Ouija board to be more than an innocent toy; incautiously used, it could open a door to troublesome entities. When Tony and his relatives sought the grandfather, there were several responses, which they at first took to be three or four distinct entities. Shortly after, though, one entity finally admitted to have been "joking," and its having been only "he" all the time, but he/it dodged early requests for his name.

This masquerading as different entities and the reluctance to give a name would have immediately raised a warning flag to an experienced metaphysicist. There's nothing wrong with an entity's having a sense of humor, but what Tony called "joking" is better described as teasing or baiting, and a proper entity is never evasive about its identity.

Lacking a seasoned perspective, Tony and his relatives pushed on, persisting in their quest for a name, until finally the board spelled out "PETER DEMARCO."[2] This stunned them, because Tony's cousin was Peter DeMarco, Junior. His father had died while Peter Junior's mother was pregnant with him.

You can well imagine that this was a momentous occasion, with highly charged emotions among the whole family. Though he was not the grandfather they had sought, they were awed to have contact with one they took to be a long-dead, near-relative. During the remainder of his stay in Italy, Tony and his cousins took several occasions to play with the Ouija board to communicate with the entity "for hours at a time."

---

2. Another pseudonym.

About a month after Tony's return to the U.S., he began to miss his sessions with the discarnate Peter, so he got his own Ouija board. As Tony's letter to us related, his father didn't "believe in those things," but—since Tony thought it took two to operate the board—his father laughingly decided to try it with him. The entity professing to be the deceased Peter responded, Tony said, but his father thought it was just Tony moving the Ouija planchette, and he left the room, laughing.

Stymied, Tony went to his own room to put up the board, but he first put his hand on the planchette to, as he put it, "apologize." To his amazement, it started to move. He hadn't dreamed it could move without two operators.[3]

Surprising as this was, to his greater astonishment, he also discovered that, once one has established a connection with an opportunistic entity, it may adopt other means to manifest. It was only a week or so later that Tony was sitting in thought at his desk. There was some paper lying on the desk, and Tony absently picked up a pencil and suddenly found Peter "getting through my arm and using my hand to write." It went slowly at first. Then, as the discarnate entity grew more adept at exerting physical control, the writing came faster. Tony sat trembling and shocked. Thus, Tony was forcibly introduced to automatic writing.[4]

He hadn't consciously volunteered control of his arm to Peter. But by having repeatedly welcomed him through the Ouija board, he had given him tacit permission to "take over," upon occasion.

---

3. In our early days of exploring the Ouija board, we quickly learned that it would respond with only Marianne touching the planchette. We've used that method for our rare Ouija sessions, since.

4. Just as an entity can be allowed to use a medium's voice, it may be given control of the muscles used in writing (and moving the Ouija board planchette). The written material produced through automatic writing, like channeled speech, is the product of the entity, not of the medium.

Over time, Peter must have written several reams of material through Tony's hand, out of which came a wealth of information about him. Peter claimed to be afraid in his current state, not knowing what to do. He had been twenty and his wife was pregnant with Peter Junior when, deranged by cocaine, Peter committed suicide. He said he hadn't expected to still be "alive" (aware) once he shot himself. When he saw the Light [of the astral levels], he cowered in this realm, confused and afraid. Exemplifying that, for some, death brings many surprises!

Peter alluded to watching his son, his family, and relatives on both sides of the Atlantic grow and interact in physical time, from which we concluded that he was not a "trapped" or "unaware" soul. Peter (or whatever entity) knew he was dead, but was "afraid," for some reason, to move on. He also regretted having left the physical world and was struggling to continue interacting with it.

Tony's problem with all this was that Peter forcibly attached himself to Tony in troublesome ways. When Peter first commandeered his arm for automatic writing, Tony thought he could "release" the energy, much as he had with the Ouija board. But, to his dismay, he found otherwise. "It's as if his physical body was inside mine," Tony said, in his letter. "It was frightening, because whenever a thought entered my mind, he answered it. . . . He lied to me . . . was mean . . . but he often apologized. . . ."

This unwanted attachment probably arose from the two personalities involved. Clearly, Peter's character was less than upright, as revealed by what we came to realize was his chronic lying, and by his imposing himself on the susceptible Tony. Tony wished, on the one hand, to separate from Peter for the good of both of them. On the other hand, he appeared (from some personal details he shared with us) to have some need in his own psyche to cling to his association with Peter. Yet, at the intellectual level, Tony recognized the need to separate; thus, he appealed to us. How could we refuse?

Tony was a slight young man, unprepossessing and soft-spoken. We—Marianne, our friend Charles Strickland, and myself— spent a few minutes discussing and clarifying some of the key points in Tony's letter, and updating ourselves on events that had occurred since Tony wrote it. Was Peter, we asked, still harassing him?

"Yes," he responded. "I know he's [still] with me over half the time."

He went on to tell how he had to get used to Peter's presence, of having no privacy, of how ". . . he just holds on."

Tony admitted he had continued to use the Ouija board to communicate with his nemesis, prompting us to discourage its further use. As Charles put it to him, "[Using the Ouija board] is like calling out to 'anybody that wants to come by,' and there are always some floating around. It's been my experience that they are rarely what they claim to be. I recommend throwing the board into your fireplace, when you have a fire."

We asked about physical manifestations, and Tony told us about his TV turning on and off by itself, perhaps twenty times in a month; of doors opening and closing; and of a crucifix on the wall that kept moving around.

It was time for the business at hand. "What do you *really* want to accomplish, at this point?" I asked.

"For him to detach himself from me."

Knowing that sometimes a person's intellectual choice conflicts with some obscure emotional need, I started to say, "If you've got any part of you that wants to keep this entity . . ."

"No, I'll be completely happy if he leaves permanently."

Given this assurance, we took a few moments, as we usually do to "first timers," to explain the channeling process we were about to begin. Then Charles invoked the ritual protective field about us, and Marianne settled into trance.

Shortly, Marianne's hands began the usual tactile exploration of her body. Mainly for Tony's benefit, I explained, "The energy is feeling a different body . . . trying to acclimate to it." Then, to the emerging personality, "Good evening."

It didn't answer; instead Marianne's body began to writhe and squirm, as though the visitor found it uncomfortable. "Why do you struggle?" I asked. "Would you speak to us?"

Marianne's hand suddenly shot forward, striking the microphone I was holding in front of her. There followed a long silence, as her hands returned to their tactile exploration.

"Yes, you're in the physical," I confirmed, "in a body you're not accustomed to. You're borrowing it very briefly, so we may communicate with you directly."

Another long silence, while the entity chose not to speak. "Would you do us the honor," I insisted, "of saying 'hello,' and identifying yourself—among friends?"

Sometimes an external entity has to make several tries, before it can master speech in the strange body. After Marianne uttered some exploratory squawks, a prolonged, undulating, dirge-like groan, and a series of labored, unintelligible attempts at words, I suspected the entity could now talk. I asked, "Will you speak to us now?"

"What do you want?" The question was hoarsely whispered.

Contact! "We would like first if you would identify yourself, please."

The tone turned surly. "Who do you want?"

OK, why not cut to the bottom line right now? This one already knows he is dead. "We would like you to . . . find the light, if we can help you—if we can put you at ease," I ventured. "But I would like a name by which to address you, please."

It was little more than a murmur: "Peter."

"Peter?" I repeated. "Are you telling me you are indeed Peter DeMarco?"

He mouthed a soundless "Yes."

"All right, Peter DeMarco. May I ask why you are on this plane?"

"To watch. . . ." The voice trailed off.

"To watch?" I asked. "Are you here by choice? Do you feel that this plane is a better place to be than the higher planes to which you could go, if you only would?"

"Yes," he said, as if in a dream, "to watch. . . ."

"But what is the benefit in watching? Explain that to me, please."

"To see. . . ." He spoke hesitantly. "To watch the boy grow." It wasn't clear if he meant Tony or Peter Junior.

"But," I argued, "you know you can do that from the upper levels any time you choose. Are you not aware of that?"

"I don't choose!" he retorted.

Just as Tony had told us. "So I understand," I said, "but I think you don't choose for other reasons. Is it not true that you get some vicarious gratification from manifesting—inappropriately— in this young man? Would it be true to say that?"

"No!"

"No?"

"No."

The dialog was deteriorating fast. I pressed on: "I suggest to you that *that's* the reason you're staying here."

"Wrong," he said, in a singsong.

"Wrong? Give me a better reason."

Abruptly belligerent, Peter snarled, "I don't have to give you anything. . . . And I won't!"

"Aha! Now the true character comes out," I observed. "The young man [Tony] is here; would you like to speak to him?

Directly, rather than through automatic writing, or the Ouija board?"

"He knows me. . . . What should I say?"

"Maybe you should explain to him . . ." A gutteral growl intruded here, before I could say, "Why you interfere in his reality and his life."

"He *invited* me. . . ."

"Oh, he did? Have you not also interfered, at times, when you were *not* invited?"

"That's none of your business," Peter said, coldly.

I took another tack: "Why are you really afraid to go on? To seek the Higher Light?"

"I choose not to," he said, emphatically.

"Are you afraid of what you'll find there?"

"That is no concern of yours," Peter snapped.

"Well, it *is* a concern of the young man here, and it should be a concern of yours," I pointed out. "And the truth of the matter is that what awaits you there is warm, kind, and loving . . . and forgiving. But first . . ."

"How do you know?" he challenged.

"You must forgive yourself," I finished. "How do I know? It is given to me to know these things," I bluffed, "just as it is given to you, if you'll but open your eyes to it."

He was contemptuous: "Talk is cheap!"

"Talk is cheap? Well, then, go on and talk to me."

A long pause, then Peter said, "*I* stand on the brink of the abyss, not you." So! Now it was clear. He thought he was destined for Hell!

It's our understanding that the concept of a literal Hell for sinners is erroneous, that every departing soul is welcome in the realms of Light. Each soul is its own judge and learns from its mistakes, through appropriate karma, or receives Grace. Conversely, an individual may make his own subjective "Hell," here or in the Hereafter, by the way he views circumstances. With this concept, I disputed Peter's position. "The abyss is in your mind. The abyss does not exist in reality, on *any* level. . . . If you'll forgive yourself . . . forgive yourself for whatever you thought was a past mistake. . . . Go for the light!"

"You are boring me," Peter sneered, "I'm going to leave."

Frustrated by Peter's intransigence, I sought help. "I invite questions from . . . Charles?"

Charles rose to the challenge. "Do you fear the truth? Do you know the Creator?"

Peter replied with a seeming irrelevance: "Tell Rhonda I'm sorry."

Charles understood instantly. It was a diversion by Peter, suddenly implying another identity by posing as a deceased in-law relative of Charles's. "No," Charles objected, "the aura is wrong— and you know that I can see them [auras]."

"I know nothing. You bore me, too." Peter's voice dripped with scorn.

"Does the truth bore you?" Charles responded.

"IN-finitely!" He caressed the first syllable. "Infinitely; there is nothing more boring than the truth. It makes me very weary."

"That," Charles said, "is because you have not *seen* the truth. Boredom is lack of thought . . . lack of creation. The Light contains both, as it contains life, which it gave you as a gift. And as you have learned, it may not be destroyed."

"WORDS! Words . . . words . . . words. . . ." Peter's voice trailed off, as Charles continued.

"Is it not true that life is not destroyed, that your consciousness remains? Is that not a fact?"

"I know nothing of facts," Peter protested.

"Does not your presence prove that you do? And that departing from the physical does not change things?"

"Many that *he* is having contact with," Peter responded with a glare at Tony, "say I do *not* exist. Therefore I must not!"

"Yet you do exist," Charles countered, "and I know that you do. You are not Peter, and you are not [Rhonda's deceased husband]."

Peter (or whoever) then tried another ploy, now addressing me. "The water is very cold, Robert; do you remember me? It's very cold."

Another diversionary attempt; he was now impersonating the soul of a close boyhood friend of mine who drowned as a young man. "You're trying again, aren't you?" I said. "You're not my friend Clyde, either. . . . No. What you are is—you are blind to the truth, willfully refusing to accept the forgiveness, the joy that can be yours—if you would but move to the Light.

"Somewhere," I rolled on, "in those higher planes are loved ones of yours, from former lifetimes, who will be there to welcome you—will be there to help you forgive yourself, because that is the only forgiving that hasn't already been done."

A silence followed, to be broken by Charles: "On that exalted plane, you may still watch anyone grow that you wish. You may grow yourself, if you wish. But you are not growing here, and you are aware of this, and you are bored, as you have said."

Another long pause, then Peter said, again, *"You* bore me."

"Does the truth bore you?" Charles retorted.

The dialog began to sound like a broken record. "Infinitely," Peter insisted.

"Then seek the Light. The Light contains all."

"You haven't convinced me-e-e-e-e." Peter went into singsong on the last syllable.

"Because I speak truth."

"And the truth bores me," Peter said, once again.

"Yet there can be knowledge, and knowledge doesn't bore; and there can be love: it is already yours as a gift."

I jumped in: "I will *dare* you to find out."

"Oh, others have tried that," Peter said, with utter contempt. "Be more original, *puleeze!*"

So much for challenging his self-esteem. Then suddenly, he addressed Tony: "And you—do you want me to go?"

Tony spoke for the first time since Peter emerged. "You've got to go to the Light."

"Why?"

There followed several minutes of oblique verbal sparring, Tony imploring him to move on, and Peter retorting mostly in non sequiturs. Finally he addressed Tony's plea. "You would send me away? In [this] world, where others don't understand you, you would send *me* away? I like it *here.*" Peter remained adamant.

Charles moved back in. "Is your existence so empty that this is the *only* way?"

"Oh, *all* existence is that empty," Peter disparaged.

"No, it's not," Charles argued. "It is all that you *see.* If you go *look* at the Light," he suggested, "and find that it is not as I have described it, then come back. . . . Or are you afraid that I *am* right? No one will force you to stay there; you may come and go as you please."

I had held my silence long enough. "Whatever you are," I said, "you are a being of free will, which means you are free to go to the Light—and, yes, you are free to leave, if that falls short of our expectations. And when you're in the Light, you're also free to visit and observe and watch the boy grow, if that's something you'd genuinely love to do. . . . You act as though we are trying to take away your free will, which we're not. We cannot. And would not dream of it."

"Go—and if you don't like it," Charles chimed in, "you can go anywhere you want to."

"There is nothing better there," Peter insisted.

"Then go look," Charles challenged. "How do you know? Are

you also all-knowing and all-seeing? Are there indeed two Gods, and you are one?"

"Yes!"

"You're wrong . . . but if you wish, you can try to prove *me* wrong: go to the Light and look."

"Others have tried that," Peter gloated. "Oth-ers ha-ve tri-ed tha-at," he literally sang, over and over, like a child trying to drown out a parent's remonstrances.

"I do believe we are going to be a child again," Charles noted. "And like most children, you know it all. And because you refuse to learn, you have the worst company of all: yourself. Which I admit would be boring."

"Convince me," Peter challenged. "It's rather nice being here in the physical."

"Well, we're not going to let that go on forever, either. That is done with the acquiescence of the one [Marianne] whose body you're borrowing. But you may not keep it against her will—we will not allow that, because that would deny *her* free will. . . . And there is some knowledge you do *not* have, that we do, but we were taught that knowledge by the Light. Now go. . . . Or are you afraid?"

"They will punish me, and I will not go!" Peter declared.

I couldn't let this to go undisputed. " 'They' will not punish you," I declared.

"They did not punish me," Charles added, "though I have done as you have [in a previous lifetime]. I chose the time of my departure from the physical, and I went to the Light. The only crime I had committed was against myself, and I forgave me, for the Creator gives me life, and gives me choice. I know of what I speak, for I've been there."

Peter disputed him. "The priest says there is Hell."

"And you are living it, my friend," Charles said. "But the Hell that you're in," he added, "is in being caught outside of the physical and outside of the Light, and that would indeed *be* Hell."

I took another turn: "You are denying another part of yourself. You deny that there is a higher part of you, your Higher Self, that is waiting for you, to forgive you at the deepest level . . . to show you the way . . . to take you to the Light. And by denying that part of *your own self*, you are making a major mistake.

"Right now," I dropped into a whisper, "if you would open your mind up, and don't go for the Light, go for your own Higher Self."

After a long pause, I asked, "No comment?"

"They will punish me," Peter intoned again, "and I will not go."

"What will they punish you for?" Charles asked.

I jumped back in. "We don't believe Hell exists, but we do believe in reincarnation. If you like it here so much, I imagine you'll come back in another body, for another chance. Why . . ."

"Your belief in the existence of Hell, or the nonexistence of Hell, does not affect its existence," Peter declared.

"As *yours* does not, too."

"Prove to me it doesn't exist," Peter challenged.

"One cannot prove a negative," I responded. "You prove to me that it does."

"*I* am the one standing on the brink of it. *I* don't have to prove it! You're asking *me* to take this step."

"Can you see it?" I challenged.

"I know it's there," he evaded.

"How do you feel?"

"Frightened!" A surprising admission for Peter.

"Then," offered Charles, "if I were you, rather than an abyss,

I'd seek Light. What would they punish you for?—what do you *think* they'd punish you for?"

"That's none of your [expletive] business!"

"Because you took yourself out of the physical by killing your-self?" Charles continued.

"Oh, *much* more!"

"Because of the gangs?" Tony had told us that Peter had hinted of an unsavory and perhaps criminal past.

"And much more."

"Yet That which has given you life has not taken it away," Charles noted, "for you still live, do you not? . . . In borrowed bodies, sometimes, but you are perfectly alive even without a body. If That which created you wanted to punish you, It would take that life away; yet It has not done it, for It has no desire to punish. It does wish for you to learn—and there's where you learn: in the Light. You can go to it, and you have absolutely free will; if you don't like the light, turn away from it. It will not force you to stay. It has given you life, and you still have it."

"What guarantee do I have of that?" Peter retorted.

"Are you not alive?"

"No."

"Are you not aware?"

"Oh, yes."

"Is that not alive?"

"No." Peter remained adamant.

"What is life? What is your definition?"

Pointing to Marianne's body, Peter said, "This is life."

"That is a physical form," Charles countered. "That doesn't last, and you know that, 'cause you've had several yourself."

"PROVE to me that what is out there is good, and I will go to it—but *prove* to me that it is good."

"What is proof?" asked several at once.

"I would see it."

"Then look," Charles said, "look up."

"I see a ceiling!"

"Close your eyes and look for Jacob." Charles had been given a name psychically (as he later confirmed) that might get Peter's attention: a Biblical name symbolic of a solid mooring in the midst of a sea of turmoil. "He's there. . . . That is one you will not distrust. Ask for Jacob. Go to the gate and ask for Jacob to come to the gate and meet you outside."

Another long pause, then Peter asked Tony, "Are *you* going to send me away?"

"You have to go."

Quickly, I added, "You go of your own free will."

"Go to the gate and ask to speak to Jacob," Charles said again. "He will come."

"Close your eyes. Go to the gate," I echoed.

"You don't have to go in," Charles assured, "he can talk to you through the gate."

"Try us," I whispered.

"*You* want me to go?" Peter asked Tony.

"You have to. Yes." It was a whisper.

Finally, Peter appeared to withdraw. "Goodbye," I whispered, "Godspeed. May you find the Light . . . and peace."

He was gone.

The actual session ran to forty-five tense minutes of roundabout, rambling, and repetitive conversation. Unlike most of the conversations in the book, this one was selectively edited to excise the worst of the repetitious argumentation.

This certainly was one of our most difficult "rescues"—if indeed that's what it was. Marianne retained some awareness of events during Peter's contentious discourse and found them troubling. She relates:

It was one of the less comfortable channelings I've done. Peter was a Spirit aware, and I have some recollection of [his energy]. Peter was a manipulator, and I wasn't happy with Peter using my body. It took much reassurance from [her SC] that it would be OK. I didn't trust Peter's energy. It *was* a very manipulative energy, and I don't like having something coming through me that I feel is going to lie, as I believe Peter did.

He was a very unhappy camper who felt life had ill-used him, and he was going to "get back" at it one way or another. And Tony, somewhat unhappy and needy of attention, was a perfect victim for Peter's manipulations. I don't feel it was a successful release.

I feel [Jacob's] energy coming through Charles was very sincere, but I don't think it was successful, and I think Peter kind of manipulated all of us into thinking it was, to get us off his back.

While we'd prefer to think Jacob did in fact entice him to leave this plane, in light of Peter's character, it's probable that Marianne was right: he only *pretended* to us that he went. Tony, in a later communication, said he had occasionally felt some of the old "Peter's here" sensations since our session, but he carefully ignored, rather than welcomed, them. If Peter in fact did not leave, at least he's no longer living vicariously in our reality through Tony. On the other hand, Peter was repeatedly promised he could return as a visitor, should he choose; perhaps he did. Either way, we understand he is no longer injecting himself into Tony's thoughts and actions, and troubling his life.

There is a more fundamental uncertainty in this case: *Was this entity truly Peter DeMarco?* Or was that just a convenient role assumed by some opportunistic being to take advantage of Tony's invitation through the Ouija board? Marianne believes it was; but consider that during Tony's initial contacts, it pretended to be three or four unidentified entities, and, during our session, it attempted to impersonate deceased souls known only to Charles or to me. You'll recall that Charles once directly accused, "You are not Peter . . . ," and the entity didn't refute him. Given this proclivity for deception, we can't say with certainty that we were dealing with the "real" Peter; yet such deception may well be consistent with Peter's character in life. Barring further information to the contrary, we accept that we were dealing with the real Peter, and that he did go to Jacob—at least to look.

This case has two distinctions: first, the subject soul was not unaware; Peter knew he had died, but remained on this plane because he was afraid of punishment in Hell. Second, he was *attached* to a living person because, being aware of events occurring in present physical reality, he sought to participate in it through Tony. (The "unaware" entity, on the other hand, is locked perceptively in the moment of its impending physical demise, where time and events are frozen. Being blind to present reality, the "unaware" soul has no concept of attachment to a person physically living in the present.)

This matter of attachment to a living person raises a question: can an attached entity exert some control over the host person, against the host's will? You will recall Melinda, the reclusive child-energy attached to the household of Jim and Cheryl in Arlington. We never fully established if she were truly unaware, and we didn't "rescue" her. In any event, there is no evidence she exerted any external influence on their lives. But, of course, hers was not an aggressive personality.

It has long been our contention that an external entity can exert only as much influence as the host allows; yet certain statements in Tony's letter lead one to wonder: "I felt half my normal energy. . . . It was as if his physical body was inside mine." He went on to say it was hard to think clearly, and he couldn't enjoy food because it was like eating paper. At times, Peter mischievously would wake him several times during the night. It was a highly fearful time for Tony.

Clearly, Peter impacted negatively on Tony; what isn't clear is whether Tony may have—at some level of mind—invited such attention. We do know that he came to view Peter as a companion of sorts and had strongly conflicting feelings about releasing him.

We have more recently had discussions with certain others involved in entity-releases, and their experience suggests that some living hosts to attached entities are subtly, subliminally influenced by those entities in their emotions and thinking, *even when the hosts have no knowledge* of those entities. (Bear in mind that Tony was aware of Peter.)

Supporting this concept, in her book, *Unquiet Dead*,[5] prominent American psychologist, Edith Fiore, concluded that a large percentage of the thousands of subjects she regressed had one or more "attached" spirits. Though the subjects were unaware of them, she alleges these attachments often influenced their hosts in varying degrees, some approaching actual possession, though not necessarily *demonic* possession, in its classical sense.[6] (This topic is considered further in the final chapter.)

5. Edith Fiore, *The Unquiet Dead* (New York: Ballantine Books).
6. Our experiences include what was a temporary but convincing possession by an entity that was maliciously arrogant, though probably not truly demonic. This differed from entity "attachments" in that the host's consciousness during the incident was totally displaced, (leaving no memory of the episode) by the intruding personality, who also usurped complete, violence-threatening bodily

In view of the evidence for attachment and—rarely—full possession, we no longer say with absolute certainty that ghosts can never harm one, but neither do we advocate fearing them—for fear itself may empower them. After all, if reincarnation is fact, we've all been ghosts ourselves.

---

control. In this instance, though, there is reason to believe the host inadvertently invited the visitation, in part by overindulgence in alcohol (some incorporeal entities seem to be drawn to heavy drinkers or other substance abusers), and by rashly issuing a challenge of sorts to the astral realm.

13

MISSIONS AND REWARDS

Through the pages of this book, you've witnessed our sometimes blundering, sometimes serendipitous steps on the road to better understanding discarnate personalities. By now, our experiences exceed the few detailed in this book. Several successful releases were not tape recorded, while still other sessions were more emotional than verbal—like Eliza's—and do not transcribe well into print. But, apart from the "novelty" of speaking with deceased entities, is there any possible merit—some worthwhile result—to our activities?

Along with Roger Pile, we consider "rescue" of unaware souls a beneficent objective unto itself, even though aiding them, one individual at a time, may be like draining a lake one drop at a time. But there are other, tangible benefits that may result, as well. Examples are the need for the drowned Evan to convince his mother to release him emotionally, so he might go on, which, if successful, presumably helped both him and his mother; and that Tony needed to sever Peter's attachment to him, again a service to both, were it successful.

In addition to whatever benefits may come from "conventional" channeling of deceased personalities, as described in this book, psychics also assist the police more than the general public knows. When it's suspected that a missing person may have met death, or there has been an unsolved murder, a psychic's supposed ability to establish an intuitive or psychic link with the victim may—at least sometimes—provide leads for police to develop.

A few years ago, when Marianne thought she might discern some useful clue in connection with a missing child, we wondered how the local police would respond to a self-avowed psychic. To our considerable surprise, they listened politely, without ridiculing or disdainfully dismissing our offer out of hand. We were told that information volunteered by psychics was not unusual and was always considered, even if it's rarely helpful. (As it developed, her psychic impressions in this case, accurate or not, would have been too late to save the child.)

We later learned that delving into violent crimes risks severe stress on the psychics involved. In one local murder case, Marianne sought to connect with the surviving essence of the female victim, hoping to receive a visualization of the murderer through the victim's eyes. We were in a friend's apartment, quietly watching, as Marianne went into trance, when suddenly she rent the silence with a bloodcurdling scream. The traumatic intensity of experiencing the victim's own terror instantly forced Marianne out of trance, badly shaken, and it took her many long minutes to regain her composure. She later was able to describe her perception of the killer's face to a police sketch artist.

At this session, Charles Strickland also went into trance, seeking to probe the consciousness of the unknown murderer in the hope of discerning something of his identity or location. Charles was unprepared for what happened: he literally seemed to enter the consciousness of the murderer, perceiving his thoughts, emotions, and, above all, his psychotic aberrations, as though they were Charles's own. Finding this devastatingly discomforting,

Charles disengaged quickly—but not soon enough to avoid leaving him emotionally sickened for the balance of the evening.

Later, groping for words to describe this melding with the murderer's mind, Charles suggested how one might feel if he found himself holding a weapon and standing in a circle of poisonous snakes, all coiled and poised to strike. "The thrill of danger and the urge to kill—not from fear, but utter revulsion—" he said, "pushed my adrenaline to a nearly intolerable level. His mental state was a hideous mixture of hate, fear, and compulsion, with a sickening viciousness and conflicting desire to both embrace and choke the objects of his rage—his targets. He was drawn to his crimes like the proverbial moth to the flame."

Finding experiences in psychic exploration of crimes to be unduly distressful, and seeing little evidence that whatever information we obtained was beneficial to police, we concluded that crime investigation was not one of our missions. Having thus decided, it was disturbing for Marianne to later psychically "receive" a mission[1] to "release" three local female victims of a serial killer, victims whose deaths were so violent, sudden, and traumatic that they remained on this plane in continuous torment. We certainly were reluctant to take this on; yet we understood we are never given a challenge beyond our abilities to cope with,[2] so in deference to the SC's, we dutifully set up a session.

For this, we omitted the usual approach of directly seeking

1. Subliminal nudges from one's Higher Self for acting on some transcendental agenda formulated by the SC come in various and sometimes devious ways. Perhaps most commonly, one is hit by an unexpected urge—perhaps even a nagging one—to undertake some action that hasn't been thought of or seriously considered at the conscious-mind level.

2. Thus far, this has proven true for us, with respect to such "missions" initiated by the Higher Selves involved. However, this assurance doesn't necessarily extend to challenges that one may elect to confront at the conscious level. Ego and conscious free will certainly can lead one to rash and risky actions in the psychic realm, as readily as in material reality.

from channeled entities the circumstances behind their predicaments; the alleged killer was already in custody, and we knew
from local newspaper accounts all we needed to know about these
victims. It was agreed that I would ask no questions of any of
them; I would merely attempt to calm them enough for them to
glimpse the Light and respond to loved ones coming for them.
Our hoped-for goal was to penetrate their single-minded fear for
their lives, at least momentarily, and to direct their attention to
the Light, so they might be drawn to the appropriate realm.

Before Marianne entered trance, we reviewed the victims'
names, as we understood them from newspaper accounts. Then
we set up a protective energy configuration, such as we've used
with others. Marianne began her trance induction, and the rest
of us waited anxiously.

When it was clear that she was under, I opened our first
invitation. Softly, I said, "We would now make this opportunity
for Lucy . . . to make the necessary move to be joined by loved
ones of hers that have gone on and are waiting for her . . . to
comfort her, after a very difficult, fearful experience that is now
behind her. . . ."

"Daddy! . . ." I was interrupted by the panic-stricken shout of
a threatened young woman reverting to a childhood plea for the
safety of her father's arms. "Daddy, please help me! Daddy . . .
Daddy, make him go away—PLEASE, Daddy."

Making no pretense of being her father, I continued with the
tone of a friend. "Lucy . . .," I said between her terrified sobs,
"It's all over."

She kept gasping in fear. I told her, "There's someone waiting
for you to take you—look! Look, Lucy. . . . Look! There's someone
waiting for you."

Suddenly she stifled a sob to exclaim, "Grammy!"

"Grammy! There she is," I exulted. Lucy quieted, and, sensing
she was leaving, I bade her, "Goodbye, and Godspeed."

Well! One down, two to go. Would they move through as mercifully and quickly? "Now," I said, "we would invite Cynthia, if she is ready to make this transition . . . to meet those who are waiting for her."

Silence. I prompted, "Cynthia?"

Suddenly came gasping yelps of breathtakingly intense fear. I tried to make myself heard above them. "Cynthia . . . it's all right. . . . It's over. . . . It's done."

She was moaning so copiously that I wasn't sure she heard a word. "There's someone waiting for you," I said. "Look!"

Her panting moans slowed. Perhaps my entreaties were penetrating her obsessive state. "Look," I whispered, "who do you see?"

She said nothing, but gave what I took to be a sigh of recognition and relief. Quieting, she seemed to find peace, and withdrew before I could offer my usual parting benediction. I felt we'd managed one more successful "rescue."

Things seemed to be on a roll, so on with number three: "And now, Martha," I invited, "the invitation is open. The time has come for you to leave physicality behind. It's already happened.

"You need to adjust," I explained to her silence. "You need to recognize that there are loved ones waiting to greet you . . . in this new existence. What's done is done; the pain is gone."

This time there were no screams, no wails. Martha just whispered breathlessly from the twenty-third psalm: "'Yea, though I walk through the valley of the shadow of death'—please get this done with fast!"

"Yes. . . ."

She repeated from the psalm. "'Yea, though I walk through the valley of the shadow of death, I will fear no evil. . . .'"

"It is up to you," I whispered, "to put this behind you. The evil is behind you."

"Please," Martha implored, "Oh, Jesus!"

"There is someone waiting to greet you now," I assured her. "Please look.

"The evil is past ... the evil is gone," I insisted. "It's all over. ... It was difficult, but it's done."

She still dwelt in the comfort of the psalm: "'Though I walk through the valley ... '"

I joined in: "'The Lord is my Shepherd; I shall not want. . . .' And He, and loved ones, are waiting for you. Please join them."

A pause, then her tone brightened. "Hello, Granddad," she greeted with relief. "Please take me. Please."

"Thank you, Granddad!" I said, relieved. To Martha, "Goodbye! Godspeed!"

It was over.

So what we feared might be exceedingly traumatic for us, as well as for those we pointed to the Light, turned out to be quick, bearable, and gratifying, in the end. We thanked the Higher powers for easing our mission.

Not that it was a piece of cake. Marianne said afterward, "I was mercifully not 'with it' during the releases, but I was certainly aware, as my body was being filled with their energies, of total and complete terror before I was kind of anesthetized. They died in an absolute height of terror, of pain, of degradation of things done to them sexually—these women died just absolutely horrible deaths and were so very much caught in their moments of death. I feel like these were successful releases, although [I concede] that may be just wishful thinking."

Are ghosts always a liability? Must we always help them and those they afflict? In this book, we've met ghosts that require our help to move on, and ghosts that trouble people by becoming attached to them, and even ghosts that mean well, but whose inept manipulation of physical objects makes them more nuisances than help. Are there beneficial ghosts?

We know of several and have conversed with one. Her name is Agnes (*not* the Sister Agnes of Chapter 7), and she reigns at Oakley, the country estate mentioned in earlier chapters, at which our friend, Georgia, was caretaker for a time.

Oakley was settled in the 1800s by a Doctor Frederick Wills, who erected a small office building a few hundred feet from the main residence, in which he conducted his medical practice. Of his son, we know little, but his daughter, Agnes, grew up to assist the doctor in ministrations to his patients.

On one of our metaphysical group outings to Oakley, the atmosphere seemed so comforting and tranquil we decided to psychically explore the energies there. Marianne was the first to go into trance and manifest her Higher Self. He reported:

> There's an abundance of warmth and happiness here at Oakley, a lot of it due to the love and care that Doc Wills gave to this property. His spirit certainly continues to reside here and still acts as a healer to those who come. The spirits of those who visit Oakley are soothed and made tranquil again. It's a healing spot for troubled people. And that healing is due to the therapeutic warmth and happiness that surrounds Doctor Wills and all of the spirits that are working in and through Oakley.
>
> He prefers not to communicate directly through a channel—the reason that I'm given for that is he would have a great deal of difficulty laughing through female vocal cords; the sound wouldn't be right! But he is responsible for the warmth and happiness that you all feel surrounding yourself here today.

I asked about the use of the present tense.

He is still here ... he's still working with people who come to Oakley; he's still healing, but he's healing troubled spirits instead of troubled bodies now.

I then asked about Agnes, of whom we already know.

A former resident of the house, and she is one of the spirits that works with Doctor Wills in his mission here. Very pleasant, a healer herself. There are no threatening entities here; there's only love and warmth and tranquillity to be found at Oakley.

Well, if Doc Wills declined to converse directly with us that day, perhaps Agnes would? I noticed Sandie had unobtrusively slipped into trance state. I probed for Sandie's Higher Self: "Hello?"

"[Sandie's Higher Self] has graciously stepped aside, so that I could say a few words to you."

"And who? ..." I started to ask.

"I am Agnes," she said. "I would like to tell you that I'm so pleased you're all here. It's been such a long time since I have felt the need to communicate, and an even longer time since there has been the opportunity.

"We are," she continued, "all very pleased that you could be here to share the peace that we feel here. When it was first made known to us that you would be here, we felt that you would certainly appreciate the higher-level aspects that you would find here."

The sound of birds filled a pause here, while we waited for more from Agnes. "I have no messages for you; I only wish to again welcome you, to thank you for being here."

"Well," I said, "we're delighted. And before you go away, I expect Georgia has a lot of questions."

Georgia pondered this, then finally said, "No, it's just like suspicions confirmed. I felt the presence—oh, ever since I've been here, and I guess my question again would be, is there something that I'm missing . . . that I need to be conscious of? It seems to me sometimes that things are not moving in the right direction here; that I need to start *something,* and I don't know what it is."

"Most of the time," Agnes responded, "when you feel this, it's just mortal depression. The sense of frustration, because you have made several attempts to do things that you felt were worthwhile—not only for yourself, but for others, too. The time is coming when these veils—these shadows—will be lifted from your thinking. You have yet to truly accept your own abilities, and accept the gifts that you have—particularly in healing—that you can share with others. You have some reservations; once you rid yourself of these, you won't need to ask what you should be doing. The answers will come without asking questions."

"Thank you," Georgia said.

This seemed to end the exchange. "Thank you very much, Agnes," I said.

"You are very welcome. And please, all of you, come again."

And she withdrew.

Georgia had researched some of the history of Oakley and Agnes's role in it. Being remote from a town, the estate, in Agnes's time, had its own chapel, located across the road from the main residence. On pleasant Sunday mornings, the family would walk across to the chapel. When Miss Agnes became engaged to a local landed swain from another estate, he often rode his horse to the chapel on Sunday mornings to join the Wills family, spending the day with them, after worship. One Sunday, while the family was returning home after services, Agnes's fiancé, "showing off" for his betrothed, elected to jump his horse across the ditch beside the road. Unfortunately, the horse lost its footing, the young man was thrown, and his neck was broken.

Agnes was so devastated, she never risked another romance. She remained single and devoted to her father's practice for the rest of his days—and hers. We understand she never moved from Oakley.

In any event, she's still there in spirit, as Marianne's Higher Self said—a factor (with her father's essence) in the emotionally therapeutic atmosphere most persons feel when they visit Oakley. She's not "unaware"; she's there by choice. She is occasionally glimpsed—or heard—opening doors, or sensed in some other way.

She's a helpful ghost, even on the physical level. Fulfilling Agnes's prediction on that day in 1983 that Georgia would eventually find a direction for her drive to be of service to others, Georgia did, some months later, enter school to become a nurse. The school was some distance from rural Oakley, necessitating an early rising hour for Georgia.

As Georgia relates it, should she, for some reason, fail to set her alarm or to hear it, there would come a loud, imperious knock on her bedroom door. Since she lived alone, she concluded it was Agnes, making certain she arose in time to get to school. Truly, a helpful ghost.

But ghosts can make mistakes, too. Georgia amuses us by telling of a morning Agnes knocked on the bedroom door, as usual, when Georgia hadn't yet stirred. But this day was different. Georgia yelled, "Agnes, this is *Saturday!* I don't have classes today!" That seemed to satisfy the ghost. And she never repeated the mistake.

These interchanges with Agnes contrast sharply with those typical of "unaware" entities, as well as of attached entities, whose focus is on themselves and their predicaments or desires. As

Marianne says of Agnes, (versus the three serial killer victims), "Agnes is just a very lovely, hostess-y energy. Compared to her, it's very hard to contrast [the terrified three] because they're such different experiences. It's the difference between holding a warm, purring cat on your lap and being wrapped up with a python."

Rather than being self-seeking—which includes Rosie and Lizzie, as well, who stick around mainly for their own pleasure— some ghosts, like Agnes, are free to remain and work in whatever positive ways they can manage to manifest on this plane. For most of these, it's probably a challenge to find mortals who are psychically sensitive to their help.

14

A GHOST OF YOUR OWN?

Someone recently asked why I was writing this book, and I couldn't answer it succinctly off the top of my head. My broad objective, at the beginning, was to share with interested readers our first-person experiences, which I feel more strongly substantiate the personal survival of physical death than do most anecdotal reports in the voluminous literature about ghosts. However, I had to take a few moments to more explicitly formulate the several reasons which—even this late in the writing—I hadn't fully articulated, even to myself. After pondering it, I arrived at the following reasons:

1. To acquaint curious readers unfamiliar with, and perhaps even skeptical about, the reality of ghosts, with the credibility our experiences lend to their existence and, thereby, to the concept of survival of the personality beyond physical death. I believe giving public voice to these personalities—literally in their own words—rather than merely relating and perpetuating anecdotal second-hand observations, as do most books on ghost lore, greatly reinforces that

confirmation. Perhaps, while short of scientific proof, this will aid readers with a tenuous belief in, or doubt about, the survival of one's personal essence—of one's soul, if you choose—beyond physical death.

2. To introduce the existence of unaware "earthbound" souls to readers unfamiliar with the concept, in order to show that a soul's being so self-restricted isn't a rare predicament, and to suggest that, when called upon to do so, helping one to "see the light" and move on is spiritually beneficent.

3. To inform those of you who suspect you may be harboring a ghostly entity (or entities) in your own premises, that the writings here and in the Appendices provide various experienced individuals and institutions that may be called upon for confirmation and possible assistance in giving you—and the ghost—relief.

4. To underline the existence of deceitful, nonphysical energies, whether deceased human or something other. This is *not* a do-it-yourself book, but for that inevitable reader who is interested—but a neophyte—in directly exploring ghost phenomena, they must be warned against gullibility and incaution and learn the basics first.

Addressing points 1 and 2: Are the ghosts we've met here real? Not real in a tangible, corporeal sense, of course, but are they what (and whom) they appear to be: distinct, conscious entities— remnant personalities of deceased humans—inhabiting an ethereal realm that coexists with our physical reality? Are they in fact surviving personalities of individuals once alive? Personalities that, with a few exceptions, are indeed confused and unaware of the better realms that are theirs for the asking?

With respect to those in this book, our answer is "Yes." We

accept these channeled personalities to be indeed what they seem. Because most of them differ markedly from certain other popular "spirit" manifestations, such as some noted below, we take them at face value. Our confidence comes in part from reliance on a screening process: when Marianne "channels" these ghosts, displacing her own consciousness so that a discarnate personality of one deceased may temporarily function through her eyes, ears, and voice, she first requests her Higher Self to invoke a protective psychic barrier to discarnate imposters and other negative energies. And, as you've noted, we also often invoke a consciously imaged protective energy "screen."[1] It's comforting to feel we're reinforcing whatever higher-level protection we may be given, perhaps following the oft-stated admonition that "the Lord helps those who help themselves." Thus far, for us, these measures seem to have worked.

What our ghosts here decidedly are *not* are consciously fraudulent creations of the medium's own mind. Even the most perverse skeptics concede this. Then, might these "ghosts" perhaps be only alternate, dissociated personalities of the living person, unsuspected independent dimensions lurking in the depths of the channeler/medium's psyche, as some skeptics contend? As Chapter 1 noted, modern psychiatry does accept the reality of Multiple Personality Disorder (MPD), a dissociative mental aberration in which one may exhibit two or many distinct personalities existent within one's own mind. Science does not accept ghosts;

1. In her long-term bestseller, *Embraced By the Light* (Gold Leaf Press, 1992, Placerville, California; pp. 126–127), Betty J. Eadie reports how, lying at near-death in a hospital bed, what she perceived to be a protective "huge dome of light, almost like glass," was placed over her and effectively repulsed several hideous, nonhuman creatures of a clearly malevolent nature that were intent upon attacking her. She understood this was a supernatural, protective shield deployed by her guarding angels; we believe such shields can be psychically requested and reinforced by conscious visualization.

could MPD rationally account for the characters Marianne and our associates have brought forth to populate the pages of this book?

As her husband of many years, who knows Marianne well— and who also personally knows at least one genuinely MPD-afflicted individual—I can confidently rule out this explanation for the phenomena we have experienced. The ghosts of this book are transitory, one-shot visitors that briefly entered and then exited Marianne's psyche permanently; they do not take refuge in the nether-recesses of her mind to resurface, at some later time. MPD simply will not suffice for explaining the characters peopling these pages.

My exploration of the paranormal leaves me virtually no doubt that in fact there are nebulous realms populated by discarnate entities, despite the fact that we have yet to prove it scientifically.[2] And, having seen it happen many times, I'm equally satisfied that assorted denizens from one or more of these realms can, and do, "enter" and communicate, verbally or otherwise, through a mortal, physical person who has the ability and the nerve—or perhaps foolhardiness—to open themselves to being so entered. Many of these entities, if not all of them, seem to be the surviving personalities of humans who were once physically alive, some of whom don't know they are no longer mortal. It is these latter entities, their perceptual awareness frozen in the moment of their physical demise, that need to be "awakened" and convinced to move on to an appropriate level.

---

2. Many open-minded scientists have tried valiantly, over the past century, to establish irrefutable proof of paranormal reality, but have failed to do so to the satisfaction of their doubting peers. Probably the root of their frustration lies in their reliance on the instruments of physical reality to detect nonphysical reality. It's like a tribal communicator using his ears and signal drums to confirm the reality of radio transmission: It exists, but he'll never detect it within the limitations of his instruments.

The process of "soul rescue" certainly isn't original to Marianne and me. In our early exploration of metaphysics, the possibility of becoming "ghost busters" never occurred to either of us. It wasn't planned; we unexpectedly fell into it on that August night in 1982, when Angelica emerged uninvited, confused, distraught, and desperately in need of guidance. We have since learned that such "rescues" have for years assumed the role of a mission for some metaphysicians. Hans Holzer, with his psychic cohorts, is one; our friend, Roger Pile, is another. We still don't actively seek unaware discarnate souls, but as persons come to us with tales of "haunted" homes or workplaces within our locale, we're open to explore their circumstances, as our time—and their willingness—will allow. As you've seen here, we do seem to succeed, at times, in sending confused entities to their astral destinations.

This underlines the suggestion made in Point 2 at the beginning of this chapter: As I noted in the previous chapter, there is a sense of achievement in effecting a successful "soul rescue." Believing emotional distress and disorientation to be as traumatic to one on the "other" side as it was on this one, it's gratifying when we can lead a discarnate personality into escaping its self-imposed hell. And beyond the extraction of the soul from that imprisoning hell, we believe there generally awaits a higher destiny for the discarnate soul which is long overdue. Thus, we see a double benefit for the obsessed personality that can be "shown the way," so to speak. In a small, modest way, perhaps, "soul rescue" is a ministry to the deceased. Further, sending a troubled soul energy on its way is often a relief to the human(s) who were discomfited by its presence here.

If you fall under Point 3 of the chapter's opening—if you suspect your premises may be harboring some nonphysical energy, what should you do? You won't find "ghost busters" under "Pest Control Services"—or any other heading—in the *Yellow Pages*, nor does it appear often in the classified ads in the paper. Many sincere and genuine researchers of ghost phenomena and soul-release don't charge for their services (although they may accept payment for expenses, if travel and lodging are involved) and don't advertise. Where does one find help?

First, do you *need* help? Perhaps not, if, as in the cases here of Agnes and of Lizzie and Rosie, your ghost is there by choice and will listen when you speak to it. If you feel this to be the case, and it chooses to share your home and family beneficially, why drive it away? Benign ghost residents cost nothing to support!

On the other hand, some aware, nonphysical personalities seem to resent the mortals occupying "their" property and may engage in acts ranging from the annoying to the alarming. Some people report success in convincing such a ghost by speaking directly to it, telling it sharply that it must move on—or at least must leave you in peace. There's no guarantee that this will succeed, though.

If you feel that you need outside help in ridding your place of one or more unwelcome entities, consider whether you care to first discuss it with your pastor, rabbi, or priest. Some among the clergy may suggest that the cure lies in submitting yourself to psychological counseling, but others will listen more openly and may have experience with persons who have contended with similar phenomena. A word of caution: Certain rigid Christian dogmas consider *all* psychic or paranormal happenings to be, prima facie, works of the Devil. It is prudent to avoid discussing your "haunting" with individuals—clergy or other—who would jump to the conclusion—as one nationally prominent investigative pair seems prone to do—that your experiences are surely incidents of demonic activity. The controversial subject of demonic activity is discussed further in this chapter, but I emphasize here that while the entities we have introduced in this book may have had typically human foibles, there seemed to be nothing demonic or Satanic about them. This conclusion was reinforced by Marianne's aura perception, with which she saw none of them to be malevolent.

If you're not comfortable turning to one of the clergy, you may prefer to seek a psychic or metaphysical organization in your locality, with members experienced in ghost phenomena. Such organizations are often small, informal, and obscure; yet often there are groups even in small communities, though their membership may not include experienced "ghost hunters." If you know of no such organizations, look for a New Age bookstore that specializes in metaphysical, psychic, alternative-health, and self-realization books and periodicals; such bookstores often serve as central information centers for metaphysical organizations.

If you do locate and turn to such a group for help, proceed carefully. Although there are a few individuals with academic degrees in general parapsychology, there's no accrediting or certifying organization that tests and awards credentials to layperson ghost busters, per se. Should you locate an alleged, but uncredentialed, ghost-communicator, ask for the names of others he or she (or they) has helped with similar problems. Inquire of those references whether he or she seemed genuine and effective. Above all, do *not* go to those professional practitioners who blatantly advertise removal of a curse or the exorcism of evil spirits. Their fundamental motive is the removal of some of your money; some wouldn't recognize a real ghost if it suddenly spoke through their own lips.

Failing all of the above, if you have a haunting that persists, that is a nuisance or even a seeming threat, you can resort to one of the organizations that are scientifically dedicated to detecting and communicating with ghosts. A few rare universities have, or have had, parapsychology departments.[3] A few others have one or more faculty members of their psychology departments open to and experienced in the paranormal. Today, the most prominent, scientifically credentialed investigator of the paranormal—including ghosts—is Loyd Auerbach, who is now director of the Office of Paranormal Investigation[4] (and Psionics Consultants), an organization established in 1989 to provide investigative, consultative, and educational services to the general public, the scientific community (in and outside of parapsychology), and the media. An alternative, but indirect, contact route is to address him in care of one of his publishers: Warner Books, Inc., 666 Fifth Avenue, New York, New York 10103. (He suggests enclosing a stamped, self-addressed envelope with your query.)

In the back of his books—*ESP, Hauntings and Poltergeists,* and *Reincarnation, Channeling and Possession*—Auerbach lists institutional and individual sources of possible help with paranormal phenomena. (The earlier book dates to 1986, and some of the individuals listed have since retired.) Auerbach is himself a member of The Parapsychological Association, Inc.,[5] an organization of academically credentialed members associated with various universities, one or more of which may be conveniently accessible to you. While not all these individuals personally do field investigations, they may be able to refer you to field researchers of known

3. Loyd Auerbach earned the first graduate degree in parapsychology from an *accredited* institution, John F. Kennedy University, in Orinda, California. JFKU is no longer awarding such degrees. However, I understand graduate degrees in parapsychology are now offered in northern California by Rosebridge Graduate School in Concord.

4. The Office of Paranormal Investigations, P.O. Box 875, Orinda, California 94563–0875. Phone: (415) 553–2588. Like many other credentialed organizations, OPI does charge for investigative services.

5. P.O. Box 12236, Research Triangle Park, North Carolina 27709. Phone: (919) 688–8241 (as of 1992). The Psychological Association is affiliated with the prestigious American Association for the Advancement of Science.

integrity. This may be your best source of interested, individual researchers.

As for dedicated institutions, one of the earliest still survives: The American Society for Psychical Research,[6] spawned in 1885 by the even older Society for Psychical Research in England. The ASPR can provide a comprehensive and up-to-date list of organizations dedicated to serious counseling and research into paranormal (including ghostly) phenomena. Perhaps Auerbach's Office of Paranormal Investigation is your most promising initial institutional resource. However, if you're looking for sources of information, or research groups closer to you than Orinda, the ASPR may be a good source for a listing of other organizations. Also, Auerbach highly recommends The PSI Center[7] as a source of comprehensive information about both research and popular literature. Appendix 1 of this book contains a brief listing of organizations specifically offering investigations of "hauntings."

Now for Point 4: If you've come, through direct experience or study, to accept the reality of discarnate populations in nonphysical realms, and, despite some risks, you are led to investigate them yourself, either to advance your knowledge or to minister to the unaware, earthbound ones, begin by first learning the basics of metaphysics and the works of others who have preceded you. (See Appendix 2 for a bibliography of informative references.) But be wary.

Also examine your motives. If you really want to assist souls in distress and increase your metaphysical knowledge regarding discarnate entities, then proceed with due care. But if you're

6. 5 West 73rd Street, New York, New York 10023. Phone: (212) 799–5050 (as of 1993). The ASPR is a membership society with a library, newsletter, journal, and other publications, and also sponsors and conducts investigations of paranormal phenomena.

7. PSI Center (Parapsychology Sources of Information Center), 2 Plane Tree Lane, Dix Hills, New York 11746 (as of 1992).

looking for some sort of esoteric guidance—a supposedly more knowing personality to which to subjugate your free will, don't look to ghosts! You may be misguided.

I speak, with reason, of impersonators, interlopers, opportunists, and other misguided entities. I've advised before: There are as many imposters and opportunists on the "other side" as are in our physical reality. An individual's character flaws aren't eliminated by death; a scoundrel in life may remain a scoundrel in the astral realm.

Caution is in order here, but testing the spirits to confirm their identities and motivations isn't as simple as it may seem. Most of us who accept the existence of discarnate entities rarely have the time or means to mount exhaustive research to test a given spirit's validity. As you have seen, the necessarily limited efforts we've made in confirming the actual past existence of some as mortals we've interacted with have fallen tantalizingly short of explicit proof in every case.

One who has done extensive historical research on channeled entities claiming past mortal existences is Joe Fisher, a British-born Canadian who is credited by some as an expert on afterlife. He has gone to remarkable lengths, including several transoceanic trips, attempting to validate previous mortal existences in recent historical times alleged by a number of channeled discarnates who regularly "came through" to be members of a group in Canada. His book, *Hungry Ghosts*,[8] recounts his experiences in that group and the depth of his efforts to substantiate the claimed past-mortal life credentials of certain self-styled "guides" who came forth to them. It's a troubling revelation of how several channeled entities of his group's experience mixed specific, detailed, and accurate historical information (which, upon superficial research, would

---

8. Joe Fisher, *Hungry Ghosts, An Investigation into Channelling and the Spirit World* (London: Grafton Books, 1990).

seem to confirm their authenticity) with fictitious or inaccurate details. These emerged from Fisher's intensive follow-up research on-site in England and Greece, and they were all discredited. The book is recommended reading for those who would structure every detail of their lives on the guidance of one unauthenticated discarnate guide or other.

One characteristic common to Fisher's ghosts should have immediately raised a red flag regarding their authenticity: it's clear from his account that the discarnate entities enjoyed subverting their charges' free will to their own whim and control, and had no compunctions over claiming whatever fraudulent credentials they felt gave them the stature to lead—or mislead— their dupes. They encouraged ever more frequent sessions, so they could vicariously partake of their beloved physical reality with ongoing regularity. And even after *every one* that Fisher checked out proved to be deceitful, or at least erroneous on various vital details, some group members still stubbornly refused to discredit them.

It's important to emphasize here that, in contrast to *our* prime focus in the events related in this book, the purpose of Fisher's mediumship group was not to "rescue" unaware, earthbound souls, and none of the episodes he describes fits that category. Rather, they were seeking "guides" from the astral levels from whom they might gain exalted knowledge and ongoing guidance for their daily activities, and perhaps some insights into their own presumed past lives. Contrast this with "our" ghosts, most of whom were ignorant of their immateriality and who, once brought to awareness, had no attraction to physicality. (The already aware ones, such as Rosie, Lizzie, and Peter, excepted.) Other than Peter, whose character in fact somewhat resembles those of Fisher's ghosts, none of our ghosts took opportunistic advantage of an available channel to visit time and again, or posed in self-aggrandizement as a transcendental guide. There would seem little motivation among our ghosts to practice deceit (again, excepting Peter). This lends authenticity to our ghosts' identities being what they seemed.

Fisher and his group were seeking esoteric knowledge and personal direction from the channeled souls and acting on what they were told. Such yielding control of one's personal decisions to a guru—mortal or discarnate—is the mark of a cultist and an abdication of the personal responsibilities we're supposed to cultivate in this lifetime. Such relinquishment of personal power and responsibility can be found among the adherents of some of today's most touted "spiritual" gurus, such as Ramtha, Seth, Michael, Lazaris, Dr. Peebles, Blavatksky's Koot Hoomi (or Kouthoumi, or Master Kuthumi), certain Space Brothers, and the avowed source of A Course in Miracles, to name just a few.

Many persons look upon these noted entities as infallible sources of cosmic wisdom for whom such persons forsake their own judgment and free will. But are these discarnate entities in fact who or what they profess to be? How can you check, since most claim their past physical existences, if any, to be so remote in time that historical confirmation or refutation of their claims is impossible.

The tendency of opportunistic discarnates to deceive and manipulate their believers—such as with Fisher's group—justifies the Old Testament's dire prohibitions (e. g., Deuteronomy 18, 10–12) against astrologers, witches, diviners, wizards, and necromancers. Who, among the unsophisticated peoples of the time, could distinguish deceitful spirits from valid ones? It took John, in New Testament times, to soften this rule—to credit people with discernment and free will—by replacing the traditional prohibition with a milder warning: "My dear friends, do not believe all who claim to have the Spirit, but test them to find out if the spirit they have comes from God. For many false prophets have gone out everywhere."[9] In other words, not every channeled entity, including those claiming to be exalted masters or guides, is what it professes to be; yet John, when he says testing is permissible, implies there are well-motivated ones to be found.

But does even a "good" one merit utterly blind acceptance of, and adherence to, every oracular word and maxim, forsaking one's own judgment and free will? It's probably not inaccurate (nor sacrilegious) to label the contemporary adherents of the revered Jesus and His disciples—a minuscule group whose generations of followers have singularly influenced the entire Western world during the ensuing centuries—as cultists.[10] Regarding Christ to be the embodiment of God, they wholeheartedly subordinated their own judgment and free will to His incisive leadership.

As some followers still do. Like other major religions of the world, Christianity has spawned numerous factions that practice differing degrees of rigidity in adherence to Church dogma, as it has been interpreted and handed down. And in common with those other religions, ironically, its symbol has adorned the banner under which religious "enemies" have been perceived, brutal wars have been waged, and cultures destroyed, all in appalling contrast to the essence of Christ's own message of tolerance found in, for example, the Sermon on the Mount: "But I say unto you which hear, Love your enemies, do good to them. . . ."[11]

The earthly purpose of any religion is to define a common structure of social interaction that enables all mortal humans to live in peaceful and benevolent coexistence. But a guru follower mentality condemns all who fail to adhere to some misguided,

9. I John 4:1 in *Good News for Modern Man* (American Bible Society, 1971).

10. The broad meaning of "cult" is simply a particular system of religion or worship, but I use it here in its modern connotation of a group committed to intense devotion and subservience to a self-proclaimed authority figure.

11. Luke 6:27, et al.

194

narrow, and exclusionary doctrine that the cultist unthinkingly and subserviently embraces as absolute transcendent truth. This conviction precludes cultists' acceptance of disbelievers in their doctrine as equally worthy and God-favored. In their view, God forbid that an individual might exercise his free will and his intellect to find his own route to enlightenment!

A restrictive theology thwarts the peaceful and benevolent coexistence of mankind that religion should foster. American Protestant fundamentalism, for example, generally deifies selected phrases attributed to Christ in the Bible as undefiled, absolute words of God—this, despite their having been belatedly recorded by mortals, selectively filtered by early Church Councils, translated numerous times,[12] and interpreted by single-minded theologians and ministers—or that others of Jesus' recorded words may be quite contradictory.

Taking Christ's words to Thomas, "I am the way, the truth, and the life: no man cometh unto the Father, but by me"[13] in their literal English sense, foments a tacit assumption that those

12. Beside numerous versions of the Bible in other languages, since 1382 there have been at least fifteen English translations. "Bible Study Helps," *The Holy Bible* (New York: The New American Library, 1974.) p. 10.

13. John 14:6. While this seems literally to define, as the only path to God, an unquestioning acceptance of Christ's deified authority and abiding subservience to his commands, other passages imply otherwise. From Acts 10:34–35: "Then Peter opened *his* mouth, and said, Of a truth I perceive that God is no respecter of persons: But in every nation he that feareth him, and worketh rightousness, is accepted with him." And Jesus' own promise, in Revelation 22:12, is, "And, behold, I come quickly; and my reward *is* with me, to give every man according as his work [not his belief] shall be."

The literal sense of John 14:6 is a foundation stone for Christian fundamentalists, yet most would vociferously reject an equally literal interpretation of Christ's reiteration in John 10:34 of a phrase in Psalm 82:6: "Jesus answered them, Is it not written in your law, I said, Ye are gods?" To suggest to the fundamentalist that a human may be a god—or, in a popular New Age concept, an aspect of God—is blasphemy. This must be selective literalism.

who haven't received—or haven't accepted—this admonition are spiritually disadvantaged and in need of enlightenment to find acceptance by God. Even if they're well-intentioned, this inspires among fundamentalists a proselytizing of the "unsaved"— a practice that is, at the very least, an unwarranted imposition on those targeted prospects who don't abide fundamentalism's rigid literalist interpretation.

Such inflexible dogma becomes more than mere annoyance, when its adherents seek to inject its doctrines into politics and legislation, whereby they would impose on everyone various prohibitions that nonfundamentalists and the nonreligious may find unpalatable. Certainly, in an educated and enlightened society, legislated imposition of narrow religious doctrine is not conducive to harmonious social structure. This rightly is seen by others as a threat to individual liberties—a move toward aligning government with a favored religious dogma, sect, or denomination, as has happened historically in other countries and is constitutionally prohibited in ours. And as history attests, in earlier times, entire peoples were forcibly conquered or destroyed, either culturally or literally, in the name of Christianity.

If it is accurate to say that the endless strife in Ireland is truly political, despite the popular labels for the factions, we can hope the days of concerted violence in the name of Christianity are behind us. But religious fundamentalism remains a disastrously divisive element, worldwide. In the words of Christ to his disciples: ". . . yea, the time cometh, that whosoever killeth you will think that he doeth God service."[14]

When millions of cultists abdicate their own rational judgment and free will, in blind obedience to human leaders claiming absolute knowledge of God's desire or intent, and who steadfastly believe they are carrying out God's commands against human

14. John 16:2.

"enemies" of God, they're an awesome foe to confront. Any dedicated fanatic willing—an even wanting—to die for his cause is perhaps the world's most formidable warrior.

As we're now seeing. It appears, in these waning years of our twentieth century, that a fanatically fundamentalist faction of Islam is fomenting genocide at its worst in the name of ridding the world of "infidels" and other perceived ethnic undesirables in the Middle East and in remnants of the former U.S.S.R.—with our Western world on their agenda. Temples in India are suffering at the hands of dissident religious fundamentalists there. Others of the scores of volatile skirmishes scattered around the world involve some degree of real or perceived religious undertones.

So where does one seek authentic enlightenment? The essential criterion for evaluating a proclaimed leader or teacher, whether mortal or discarnate, is: By their works (shall ye know them). A true guide—whether it's your own Higher Self or a discarnate master (or angel, or God, or whatever your perception) hovering in the astral realm for your guidance—*never* makes decisions for you. One object of this earthly lifetime is to develop and discipline one's own mortal, conscious-level free will; to learn to make socially and spiritually positive decisions. Valid guides and your own SC may help you see the options and reveal information beyond that of your physical senses and conscious knowledge, but they do *not* manipulate your life nor demand your intellectual capitulation.

So, given these doubts about channeled entities, why are we comfortable regarding the validity of the discarnates we have described in this book? Because the entities we have dealt with (with the noted exception or two) have not tried to manipulate us for their own ego gratification, and therefore would seem to have no motive or purpose to deceive. In fact, our experiences here constitute a virtual reversal of the guru role: an emerging discarnate doesn't claim to be our guide; it is we (sometimes with the passing aid of related discarnates) who are instruments of guidance to the discarnate. Since these discarnates never again are heard from, nor looked upon by us reverently and repeatedly for cosmic guidance, they have no motive—and rarely the presence of mind—for pretense.

To confirm this, we turn to our own guiding higher sources: our individual SC's, who also don't usurp our conscious free will. They confirm to Marianne, Charles, Sandie, me, and others of our circle that the entities we may "rescue" are in fact what they seem: surviving personalities of deceased mortals who are unaware of their true condition and are in need of guidance.[15] As Marianne comments, "If I don't accept our [ghosts] at face value, then I can't believe *anything* I've gotten from my SC. All of these were with his permission and his cooperation. I've no reason to think that—with the exception of Peter [and the guilelessly gregarious Rosie and Lizzie]—these souls had an agenda. I think they honestly were 'trapped' here and unhappy—or [for some] here by choice and not unhappy; for Rosie and Lizzie, it was, 'Oh, goody! Someone to gossip with!' They seemed to have no need to lie to us, but I think Peter was a manipulator and a liar. Again, if I believe in my own Superconscious I have to believe that these experiences were as they have been presented."

If the encounters detailed in this book make the "rescue" of unaware souls sound like a fascinating experiment, I would cau-

---

15. With certain exceptions, as noted. Rosie and Lizzie certainly were aware and here by choice and, while they coyly implied certain historical physical existences, they made no pretense of omniscience or guidance. Child of the Moon was also not unaware; she was merely enjoying, in a way, an extension of the physical life so prematurely ended. But the one called Peter, who parasitically attached himself to Tony to partake of ongoing physical existence—however vicariously—almost certainly was a duplicitous entity. In his own way, he (mis)-guided Tony and did his contemptuous best to deceive and befuddle us. We aren't certain Peter was who he claimed, and we suspect he did not move on.

tion you again that interaction with discarnate entities isn't something to be undertaken lightly, like an entertaining game. I've said it before, here and elsewhere, but it's worth repeating: the Ouija board, for instance, is *not* a game or toy. Unfortunately, it's sold as one but, as we've seen in Chapters 11 and 12, the Ouija board has been a doorway to more than one person's psychic torment.[16] I have warned against it in my earlier book, *Death Brings Many Surprises*, and Joe Fisher seconds it: "The Ouija board attracts earthbound spirits more readily than any other inanimate device, and those who choose to 'play' this trans-dimensional distraction run the risk of being influenced by the most devious tricksters imaginable."[17]

In this connection, it's appropriate to discuss the subject of possession. While I suggested in Chapter 12 that Peter's self-serving influence on Tony was not demonic "possession," as it is popularly understood,[18] and Fisher's ghosts did not assume possession, in Chapter 11 the subject came up again in connection with the role of the Ouija board in the alleged demonic possession that inspired *The Exorcist*. Is such possession truly a risk to those who would consort with the assorted denizens of nonphysical realms? Does demonic possession indeed exist in fact?[19]

16. It happened that Marianne's and my first encounter with a deceased personality came through a Ouija board. In our inexperienced state, we were fortunate it was a well-motivated relative; we have since learned of others—like those in earlier chapters here—who opened themselves to opportunistic and duplicitous energies through ingenuous use of the board. Only after one has learned certain psychic and spiritual protective techniques should one dabble with a Ouija board. And once you reach that stage of psychic evolution, so primitive a tool as the board is no longer expedient, anyway.

17. *Hungry Ghosts. Op. Cit.* p. 260.

18. At no time was Tony's own consciousness displaced or overwhelmed by Peter's energy; Tony was only psychically "nagged." In classic possessions, the victim is totally unaware of his environment and actions during the time(s) of possession; the invading entity exercises complete mental and bodily control.

19. See entries under "Possession" and "Releasement" in Rosemary Ellen

Pursuing this, one may first ask, Does Satan exist? For possession usually is portrayed as total psychic takeover of a hapless human by Satan, or perhaps by one of his minions.

It's the fashion, in modern New Age philosophies, to deny the very existence of Satan and other entities consciously dedicated to committing and perpetuating evil in all its guises. According to this view, what we perceive as evil, as humanly and socially negative, is nothing more than innocent error arising from human ignorance, individual- or culture-wide. Carried to its extreme, this notion makes words such as *evil, bad, wrong,* etc., misnomers for describing what is only error through human ignorance. It's interesting to note that New Agers readily embrace various concepts of benevolent, incorporeal entities—guardian angels, guides, transcendental masters, a Supreme Cosmic Intellect, etc.—but deny the possible existence of any malevolent ones.

By contrast, traditional Christianity posits Satan as a very real, superhuman entity—a fallen angel, an enemy bent on diverting humanity's devotion to God and good and heavenly destiny by capturing men's souls for the Devil through temptation and tribulation. According to this teaching, Satan and his underlings are continuously seeking to snare converts, working subliminally through incorporeal assistants and directly through human agents, both willing and unwitting. Thus, Satan is deemed the god of evil, who, in rare instances, may psychically possess (or cause to be possessed) a hapless human for evil purposes. It's well known that the Roman Catholic church performs rituals of exorcism intended to drive Satan or lesser demonic spirits out of such victims; it's not so well known that a number of other Christian denominations also have provisions for such rituals.

Guiley, *The Encyclopedia of Ghosts and Spirits* (New York: Facts on File, 1992) for a discussion of various concepts of the nature of possession.

We've had no firsthand experience with classical possession, but we have interacted with one entity that, if not downright malevolent, certainly was arrogant, overbearing, physically threatening, and abusive of the occupied host's usurped body. (It required two strong men to forcefully restrain the unwitting host from materially injuring himself.) This mercifully short session ended with the host crumpling inert on the floor for several moments before normal consciousness returned.

Having anxiously witnessed this "mini-possession," we know firsthand that not all incorporeal entities are warm fuzzies; clearly, some have agendas inimical to positive human values and welfare. Given this, it's reasonable to accept the characteristics of well-documented possession cases as evidence of true possession, though not necessarily by Satan himself—if he exists.

After all, free will is a universal attribute of consciousness, be it mortal or incorporeal, so we're not surprised to find as many different motivations among individuals on the nonphysical planes as on the material one. As others have pointed out, one's character and personality don't automatically change just because one has transcended mortality. It follows that there must be some pretty malevolent souls floating about the cosmos who, given an opening, could take highly detrimental possession of an unsuspecting mortal.[20] In this light, possession neither proves nor disproves the existence of Satan; it merely proves there are highly undesirable and opportunistic entities lurking about, able to trap the unwary. Satan aside, it is these lesser evil ones to whom

20. A traditional Christian view is that such unworthy souls are consigned to Hell upon mortal death and would not be floating about the cosmos; however, in this same vein, worthy souls presumably have moved on to Heaven (or, in some views, lie in a somnolent state of suspended consciousness, awaiting Judgment Day), so that only demonic, nonhuman spirits are accessible to us on this plane. In this view, *all* channeled entities are minions of Satan. Our observations and experiences do not support this cosmology.

the Ouija board and similar communication devices may open a channel for manifestation. (Satan, if he exists, certainly doesn't need such crude tools as the Ouija board in order to exert his influence.)

If, after all this, you seriously wish to explore ghostly phenomena firsthand, start at the bottom. Read and study the work of others, not just of those who've explored and written about ghosts, but some of the vast literature devoted to the entire gamut of paranormal phenomena. You'll find no two authors in full agreement about the characteristics of any given phenomenon, but you'll gain a broad overview of the many assorted concepts of nonphysical realities and entities. From this, you may distill your own skeletal belief concept as a starting point from which to learn and to modify these concepts into a paradigm of metaphysics with which you can be comfortable. For that's your bottom line: to accept and use what works for you.

Also, understand this elementary rule of metaphysics: *No psychic source is one hundred percent accurate.* No medium or channeler, nor their channeled entities. No mortal interpreter of recorded tradition, including the Bible, Talmud, Koran, Bhagavadad-Gita, etc. Nor, I dare say, the Roman Catholic Pope. Always apply your own rational judgment to others' assertions and your own perceptions to draw your own conclusions.

Even with these caveats—despite the hidebound disbeliever who denies *all* discarnates, and the religionist who accepts discarnates but deems them *all* to be demonic, and the researcher's truth that *some* are deceitful—on the bottom line, Marianne and I believe our ghosts in this book are genuinely surviving essences of ordinary, mortal humans. We haven't sought esoteric knowledge and guidance from these once-human beings, or past-life relationships; we've sought only to give them audible voice and the comprehension to move on, as may be appropriate. We wish them all Godspeed.

APPENDIX 1:
RESOURCE
ORGANIZATIONS

The Encyclopedia of Associations lists a considerable number of professional organizations, many affiliated with universities dedicated to analytical and statistical research on various paranormal phenomena. Some only conduct controlled experiments within the academic confines of their sponsoring institutions, but a few also mount field explorations of reported paranormal events. Field trips made in response to requests from members of the general public usually incur monetary charges.

The most recently formed and visible organization of academic professionals dedicated to the study of paranormal phenomena, including on-site investigations, is directed by Loyd Auerbach. He has expressed an active interest in hearing from those of the public who believe they have experienced haunting, apparitional, or poltergeist phenomena. His address is:

> Loyd Auerbach, Director
> The Office of Paranormal Investigations
> P.O. Box 875
> Orinda, California 94563–0875
> (415) 553–2588

The organizations below are the few found in a recent edition of *The Encyclopedia of Associations* that specifically list field investigations among their services. Listings do not specify whether these organizations include academically accredited parapsychologists.

The American Society for Psychical Research
5 West 73rd Street
New York, New York 10023
(212) 799–5050
(The first and oldest of professional American paranormal research organizations.)

The Parapsychological Association
P.O. Box 12236
Research Triangle Park, North Carolina 27709
(919) 688–8241
(A national umbrella organization for academic parapsychologists and their organizations.)

Mind Development and Control Association
P.O. Box 29396
Sappington, Missouri 63126
(314) 849–3722

Parapsychological Services Institute
Dr. William Roll, President
P.O. Box 217
Carrollton, Georgia 30117
(404) 836–8696
(Dr. Roll has been a prominent and respected researcher of the paranormal for many years.)

Parapsychology Institute of America
P.O. Box 252
Elmhurst, New York 11373
(718) 894–6564

Survival Research Foundation
P.O. Box 8565
Pembroke Pines, Florida 33084
(305) 435–2730

Ghost Research Society
P.O. Box 205
Oaklawn, Illinois 60454
(708) 425–5163

APPENDIX 2:
BIBLIOGRAPHY

The books listed below encompass a wide variety of viewpoints and experiences concerning ghostly phenomena, about which probably no two agree in every respect. They are selected from several sources, including the 1995–96 edition of the *Subject Guide to Books in Print*,[1] suggestions from other researchers, and my personal library. I've not read all, or even most, of these; among those I have, authors I consider both credible and informative include Auerbach, Caidin, Fiore, Fisher, and Holzer.

Auerbach, Loyd. *Reincarnation, Channeling and Possession*. New York: Warner Books, 1993.

————. *ESP, Hauntings, and Poltergeists*. New York: Warner Books, Inc., 1986.

Bingham, Joan and Riccio, Dolores. *Haunted Houses USA*. New York: Pocket Books, 1989.

Caidin, Martin. *Ghosts of the Air*. New York: Bantam Books, 1991.

1. *Books in Print*. New York: R. R. Bowker, 1995–96.

Downer, Deborah. *Classic American Ghost Stories*. Little Rock, AR: August House, 1990.

Edwards, Norma. *What You Should Know About Ghosts but Were Afraid to Ask*. New York: Diamond Stockton, 1988.

Fiore, Edith. *Unquiet Dead: A Psychologist Works with Spirit Possession*. New York: Doubleday, 1987.

—————. *Unquiet Dead: A Psychologist Treats Spiritual Possession*. New York: Ballantine Books, 1988.

Fisher, Joe. *Hungry Ghosts*. London: Grafton Books, 1990.

Guiley, Rosemary Ellen. *Encyclopedia of Ghosts and Spirits*. New York: Facts on File, 1992.

Holzer, Hans. *Psychic Investigator*. New York: Hawthorn Books, 1968.

—————. *The Ghost Hunt*. Virginia Beach: The Donning Co./ Publishers, 1983.

—————. *Best True Ghost Stories*. Englewood Cliffs, NJ: Prentice-Hall, 1983.

————— and Ray Buckland, ed. *Ghosts Hauntings and Possessions*. St. Paul: Llewellyn Publications, 1991.

—————. *America's Restless Ghosts*. Stamford: Longmeadow Press, 1993.

Jaegers, Beverly and Jaegers, Ray. *Ghost Hunting: Professional Haunted House Investigation*. Aries Productions, 1988. [Contact B. Jaegers through Berkley Publishing Group, 200 Madison Avenue, NY, NY 10016].

Jarvis, Sharon. *True Tales of Unknown Uninvited*. New York: Bantam Books, 1989.

—————. *True Tales of the Unknown*. New York: Bantam Books, 1990. Presumably an update of the Jarvis book

—————, ed. *Dark Zones*. New York: Warner Books, 1992. above.

Meyers, Arthur. *The Ghostly Register*. Chicago: Contemporary Books Inc., 1986.

—————. *A Ghosthunter's Guide: To Haunted Landmarks, Parks,*

209

Churches & Other Public Places. Chicago: Contemporary Books Inc., 1993.

Moody, Raymond. *Reunions—Visionary Encounters with Departed Loved Ones*. New York: Villard Books, 1993.

Smyth, Frank. *Ghosts and Poltergeists* (Volume GP of The Supernatural Library). Danbury, CT: Grolier/Danbury, 1975.

Tart, Charles T. *Open Mind, Discriminating Mind: Reflections on Human Possibilities*. New York: Harper & Row, 1989.

U.S.A. Weekend Editors. *I Never Believed in Ghosts Until: One Hundred Real-Life Encounters*. Chicago: Contemporary Books Inc., 1992.

Whitaker, Terence. *Haunted England: Royal Spirits, Castle Ghosts, Phantom Coaches, & Wailing Ghosts*. New York: Dorset House Publishing Company, 1987.

Wilson, Colin. *Poltergeist: A Study in Destructive Haunting*. St. Paul: Llewellyn Publications, 1993.